THE SEARCH FOR ADIRONDACK GOLD

THE SEARCH FOR ADIRONDACK GOLD

Ron Johnson

NORTH COUNTRY BOOKS
Utica, New York

THE SEARCH FOR ADIRONDACK GOLD

ISBN 0-925168-90-4

Library of Congress Cataloging-in-Publication Data

Johnson, Ron. 1945-
  The search for Adirondack gold / Ron Johnson.
      p. cm.
  Includes bibliographical references.
  ISBN 0-925168-90-4 (alk. paper)
  1. Johnson, Ron. 1945---Travel--New York (State)--Adirondack Mountains
Region. 2. Gold mines and mining--New York (State)--Adirondack Mountains
Region. 3. Adirondack Mountains Region (N.Y.)--Gold discoveries. 4.
Adirondack Mountains Region (N.Y.)--History. 5. Adirondack Mountains Region
(N.Y.)--Description and travel. I. Title.
  F127.A2J64 2004
  974.7'5043'092--dc22
                                      2004007646

NORTH COUNTRY BOOKS
311 Turner Street
Utica, New York 13501

To Donna, David, and Jonathan,
the fine treasures of my life

County Location of Adirondack Gold Mines/Mills and Actual/Alleged Gold Discoveries

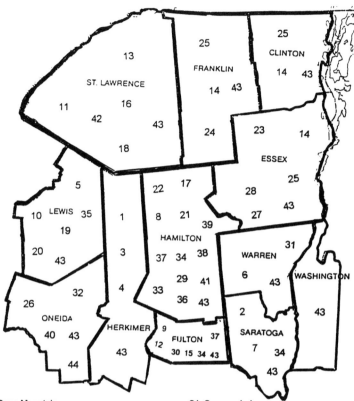

1 Ice Cave Mountain
2 Halfmoon,
3 Nelson Lake
4 Town of Webb
5 Lyonsdale
6 General ref. to Warren Country
7 Sacandaga Mining and Milling
8 General ref. to Hamilton County
9 General ref. to Fulton County
10 General ref. to Lewis County
11 Edwards, Fullerville, Fine
12 "A streambed in Fulton County"
13 St. Regis River
14 Saranac River
15 Jackson Summit
16 "Mohawk Mine"
17 Indian Lake Village
18 Parishville
19 New Breman
20 Croghan
21 West Stony Creek Gold Mine, Otter Gulch Gold Mine, and Benson Gravel/Gold Mine
22 Speculator
23 Mount Pisgah

24 Saranac Lake
25 Black Mountain
26 Ava
27 Black Mountain
28 Mount Pisgah
29 Wells
30 Bleecker
31 Hadley
32 Westernville, Boonville, Ava
33 Benson Gold Mining Company
34 Gen ref. to Fulton, Hamilton, Saratoga Co.
35 Harrisville
36 Benson, Wells
37 Caroga
38 Dug Mountain
39 Piseco
40 "Northern Oneida Coiunty"
41 "Between Lake Pleasant and Johnsburgh
42 Star Lake
43 In the Deed Abstracts of Gold Mines filed with the New York Secretary of State there are sworn affidavits about gold discoveries for every county of the Adirondack Park.
44 Boonville Gorge

TABLE OF CONTENTS

Yep, There's Really Gold in Them Thar Hills

It Glitters in Boonville Gorge

By FRANCIS L. CRUMB

Logger Stakes Claim to Adirondack Gold Discovered While Scouting Near Star Lake

By Paul Warloski
Times Staff Writer

THE PINE LOG

NEWS ITEMS FROM GOUVERNEUR

FARMER VETERAN OF KLONDIKE

Adirondack Eldorado

Scientific American

[MARCH 26, 1898.]

Adirondack Gold Tales

Gold In New York State

By ANDY MASLOWSKI

THE ADIRONDACK ELDORADO

DEVELOPMENT OF THE GOLD MINES IN FULTON AND HAMILTON

Where the Precious Metals are Found—What the Assays Show, and the Companies Interested in the Enterprise.

Introduction

In the fall of 1972 we English faculty at Adirondack Central High School (Boonville, New York) decided to conjure up a program of semester-length electives for our seniors. One of my tasks was to develop a segment in creative writing. On the official syllabus this course was titled, quite uncreatively, "WC 12," short for "Written Communication—English 12."

One covert strategy, I must admit, was to pursue writing ideas that would be robustly interesting to... me. I figured if I could maintain a contagious excitement about our various projects the odds would be that much better that I could keep my classes productively energized. A lover of North Country folklore, I therefore required every student to write an original, local color short story in lieu of a final exam. There was a hitch. Stories had to derive from some personally investigated upstate New York anecdote or legend. Apart from that, I operated with extraordinary "editorial" latitude. Source material could be recent or vintage, written or told, corroborative or fictitious, down to earth or totally nuts.

I thus became the delighted recipient of scores of stories about every imaginable topic. For example, are you aware of the way, way, way underground transcontinental aqueduct that links Lake Champlain, Echo Lake in Boonville, Kayuta Lake in Forestport, and Loch Ness in Scotland, and that this subterranean waterway explains numerous "plesiosaur" sightings of Champy, the Echo Lake Monster, the Sea Serpent of Forestport, and, of course, the Lock Ness Monster?

Have you heard about the haunted dance hall of Mohawk Hill, over in Lewis County? One night an inebriated dancer fell out a second-story window to his death. The story is that his ghost would perpetrate either funny or fiendish capers depending on whether he had last been seen ethereally waltzing beneath the north or south side of the dance hall roof.

Did you know that there is a top-secret, yet-unnamed, Adirondack swamp—utterly illusive to the United States Geological Survey—which is the source of cancer-curing, sphagnum moss?

How about the phantom railroad car of the mountains, occasionally glimpsed, but more often heard, by numerous Adirondackers as it would speed along different stretches of the Remsen-to-Lake Placid rail corridor on the blackest of North Country nights.

And so on. Unusual, intriguing stuff. And far less burdensome to correct than run-of-the-mill, inspired-while-flatlining drivel. Best of all, students had an enjoyable time experimenting with original narrative.

Some day, I vowed to myself, I'd personally get to the bottom of a few of those tales. Incidentally, the Sea Serpent of Forestport, first spotted in 1893 is thought to have been sawdust and tanbark which drifted down from the tannery on Woodhull Creek, somehow coalesced into dark glumps, and because of certain gases of decomposition, rose intermittently to the surface of McGuire's Pond (Gramps Skjellerup, however, never recanted that he and his brother once saw a monstrous "hump or dorsal fin" circle the perimeter of Echo Lake, and soundings have indicated that the lake is extremely and erratically deep). The haunted dance hall, once home to a bipolar ghost, no longer stands, but folks affirm that the building was situated in just such a way so that when it rained, water falling on the north side of the roof flowed down into the Sugar River and thence to the Black River, where it moved northerly and inexorably to Lake Ontario. Whereas rain falling on the south side of the roof drained down into the headwaters of the Mohawk River and so moved easterly and inexorably to the Atlantic Ocean. There is a widespread belief that certain Adirondack mosses do indeed have curative properties; a cobbled highrailer fitting at least one description of the phantom rail car, a '70s Olds with a cut-out roof and quick-drop front and rear speeder wheels, was impounded by the state police at Remsen a few years ago.

Among the stories crafted by my fledgling authors in WC 12 were accounts of North Country gold. A quarter of a century has passed since my trusty red pen ferreted through those tales as it sniffed out comma faults and dangling participles and misspelled words. But my curiosity about New York gold never diminished with the passing years.

In 1997, I decided to embark on a prospecting adventure. Some of the quest involved actual on-site searching—digging, picking, plucking, scooping, panning. I did most of my prospecting, though, in the literature of upstate New York. There, in newspapers and periodicals, in county histories, in the State Archives, in records of legal proceedings, in the abundance of regional interest books, I discovered a mother lode of Americana, and in the process I learned a lot about the search for gold in the North Country. It is a deep, rich vein of lore, and the claim I stake is a corporate one, bearing the names of all of us.

Geographically the adventure begins with, and ends with, North Lake, Herkimer County. Philosophically, for one cannot really talk about the pursuit of gold without touching on dreams and values and the hearts of men, my exploration begins with the words of a religious man, Father Isaac Jogues, seventeenth-century missionary to the Hurons, and ends with the words of a religious man, In Chhan, former Utican, survivor of Cambodia's killing fields, goldsmith by trade.

I have had no second thoughts about this inclusion of the serious alongside otherwise light-hearted reportage. Since my very first manuscript scribblings I sought unswervingly to produce a comprehensive account of Adirondack gold. But there is an additional component to my effort. I have obviously chosen not to be the detached, dispassionate author. What you have before you is a commentary, a transaction between reader and author, between you and me.

Consider how gazing at gold is also a kind of transaction. Gold simply has no luster absent the beholding eye. There always attends that mysterious interface between inert metal and the perceiving, processing human intellect. In the stitching together of my research, whenever I came across something that really moved me, even when quite tangential to the whereabouts of North Country gold, I purposely chose to share it with you as part of my trek. To illustrate, life in New Netherlands was not primarily a time of happy exploration, leatherstocking frivolity, and peaceful settlement. There was darkness in the land. You will glimpse that darkness, as I did. To skirt it, or excise it, in my way of thinking and writing, is to move the author-reader transaction toward the inertness of a research paper, the blandness of Introductory New York History, the tediousness of Geology 101. There is gold in them thar hills. There is also human history laced with good and evil.

While the pages that follow are an effort to straightforwardly transmit data, some of that data will be factual and verified, and other data will be patently unsubstantiated and highly speculative. A footnote and a cited, published source do not necessarily equal "substantiated." For example, I have just given you a factual account (verified by a producible orange crate full of WC 12 stories) of how I became privy to some far-fetched tales. It is a truthful transmission to you about some highly imaginative narrative, though there are apparently kernels of the authentic in some of the legends.

My desire is for readers to "romance the stones" along with me. Break out your cerebral prospecting hammers and tap away at the nuggets—or fool's gold?—of data herein. Go ahead and assay, account by account, page by page, line by line. And then you be the judge. I trust, though, that like hopeful prospectors, you'll stay positive and upbeat, lest pay dirt, without so much as one run through the sluice box, gets reduced to the mica and iron pyrite of premature skepticism. My advice? If there's room for speculation, by all means, bask in wild, unmitigated speculation, and so experience a touch of gold fever.

In their work with narrative technique my WC 12 students learned that "plot" begins with a "precipitating event." Something happens to get the ball rolling. While I offer you no plot to untangle here, you will find something of a narrative thread. This is, after all, a true tale describing my attempt to get to the bottom of accounts about North Country gold. And there was very definitely a precipitating event.

At North Lake.

Acknowledgements

I would like to acknowledge several people for their encouragement and help in this project. Certainly a word of appreciation goes to Elizabeth Folwell, *Adirondack Life*'s Editor-at-Large, who some years ago told me not to give up my day job, while simultaneously affirming my writing by publishing several of my submissions. I want to thank Fran Wilcox for his able assistance with the Americana Collection at the Utica Public Library, and for his keen knowledge of very old maps. I gratefully recall exciting conversations with the late Lewis Decker, former Fulton County deputy historian, who discovered gold—verified by the state mineralogist—in the southeast Adirondacks. I also need to thank Bob Kennerknecht, successful, professional, veteran gold prospector, who gave me pointers about panning and about the best places to look for black sand. To Ted Comstock, specialist in historical research, I offer my gratefulness for words of encouragement and for tracking down several North Country accounts of gold. Behind the nuts and bolts business of organizing this material lies the wise editorial guidance of Sheila Orlin, North Country Books publisher. For many years she has unpretentiously been, in fact, the wind beneath the wings of numerous regional-interest authors. Zach Steffen, Sheila's able assistant, deserves my thanks for preparing the final version of the manuscript. I must note appreciation for North Country Books' Rob Igoe, Jr., whose contagious confidence kept me optimistic. I am indebted to Dr. William Kelly, former New York State Curator of Minerals, who graciously let me plunder his "gold file." His words of caution, his tantalizing anecdotes, his great sense of humor, both fired my imagination and helped me keep my feet on the ground.

Finally, I thank Donna, my wife, who, on our first date thirty-one years ago, dared to hop on the back of my motorcycle with me and chug through the Adirondacks on a glorious spring day. In my heart, because of her, it has never stopped being spring.

Gold dust blinds all eyes

—Cheales

—1—

Ice Cave Creek

One of several "canal reservoirs" built in the mid-1800s to hold residual water for both the Erie Canal and the Black River Canal, North Lake is located in Herkimer County, about ten miles inside the Blue Line (Adirondack Park boundary), and is part of the Black River Wild Forest. The elongated lake is pretty much a water-filled ravine that stretches from the Atwell dam north to the base of Ice Cave Mountain. Actually, post-dam North Lake is the extended version of a previously existing Sophia Lake. Ice Cave Creek is a North Lake inlet stream.

One beautiful spring day in 1989, I took a newly acquired canoe for a test paddle on North Lake. I recall easing into the mouth of Ice Cave Creek until I felt my hull gently touch the sandy bottom. At the time there was no wind and the water was glass smooth. I remember that I was in a kneeling position just behind the middle thwart and that I stuck my paddle into the sand as a kind of prop. Steadying myself with the paddle shaft, I leaned over the starboard gunnel to study my chines—where the sides of a canoe merge with its bottom.

I was admiring the way the builder's unique hull design had allowed me to paddle in such shallow water when suddenly my eyes caught something glittering right next to the paddle blade. Then I looked on the other side of the canoe and saw four or five more specks glinting in the bright noon sun.

Hum, I thought. Must be flakes of mica.

Maybe not, the Indiana Jones down inside me protested. Maybe it's gold, washed down from some high ground to the north! After all, who really knows what treasures lie hidden in these wilderness mountains, anyway? Gold, the old timers say, is where you find it!

With both imagination and pulse now racing I popped my last Luden's Honey-Licorice cough drop into my mouth, pinched up a half dozen gold colored "samples" out of the sand, folded them into the cough

Ice Cave Mountain is just beyond the north shore of North Lake in the town of Ohio, Herkimer County. Ice Cave Creek lies at the base of the mountain's west slope and the North Branch of the Black River lies along the base of the east slope. Both of these cascading streams surely become natural mineral sluices during spring run-off.

drop wax paper, and put my find into the empty Luden's box. I then paddled the three and a half miles back to the put-in at Atwell, loaded the canoe onto my truck, and headed home to Utica. With a plan.

I would take my specimens down to Fast Eddy's Pawn Shop and see how they reacted to his all-discerning nitric acid. Fast Eddy had his assay elixir in three strengths so that he could test for 24-carat, 18-carat, and 10-carat gold. On fake gold, nitric acid produces a greenish bubble. And if you make a line on black soapstone with your test specimen, and you have something other than gold, nitric acid erases the line.

This preliminary testing was a good idea, and I would have followed through with it had Donna, my wife, not come across a damp, scrunched-up, apparently empty cough drop box and tossed it into the garbage. Thanks to Donna and the city trash haulers Fast Eddy was going to have to wait for the next trip to North Lake.

With the passing weeks, however, I became more and more convinced that I had only discovered mica, and I eventually lost interest in a second trip. Then my imagination detonated a second time. I was in the Utica Public Library browsing through a book of Adirondack stories when I came across an account of a North Lake, part-time hermit who was supposed to have found gold up on Ice Cave Mountain.

I immediately thought about my own discovery of 1989. Why, I had been at the mouth of the very creek which was surely a resting place for any heavy metal particles sluicing off the western slopes of Ice Cave Mountain. And I thought also about my orange crate full of student stories, a few of which were about lost gold mines.

It was high time for a call to the State Mineralogist, Dr. William Kelly. I reached him at the State Museum in Albany and asked him straight out, "Is there gold in the Adirondacks?" His qualified "yes" was tucked into a spirited mini-lecture about ever bewitching fool's gold and constantly resurfacing, dead-end tales about North Country El Dorados. He talked about varieties of mining quackery and secret gold-extracting processes that sounded a lot like medieval alchemy. He probably wasn't aware of it, but in twenty minutes he had given me a bevy of topics to investigate and a number of leads to chase down. As I listened I felt surges of excitement. The thrill of a great hunt was taking hold.

We are going to get back to this phone conversation later. For now I will just say that it was the talk with Dr. Kelly that catapulted me into an enthusiastic search for earliest literary references to New York gold. Finding those glimmering specs at North Lake had been a precipitating event.

Suddenly it was precipitating cats and dogs.

Hurtling through the vast silence of inter-stellar space, attached to a derelict spacecraft, is a small golden plaque bearing mankind's first message to worlds beyond the solar system. Etched on the gold surface are the naked figures of a man and a woman with their return address engraved in scientific symbols, conceivably understandable to extraterrestrial civilizations.

The plaque was affixed to the antenna support struts of Pioneer 10 when it was launched in 1972 from Cape Canaveral on a voyage that has taken it past the planet Jupiter toward a point on the celestial sphere near the constellations Taurus and Orion.

Oceanic space is vast and empty. It will take 80,000 years for the golden greeting to travel to the nearest star and more than ten billion years to enter the closest star planetary system. But because its surface is gold the six-by-nine inch plaque can be expected to remain eternally shiny and smooth, free of tarnish, scale, or corrosion.

The Magic of Gold
—Jenifer Marx

—2—

Half Moon *on the Hudson*

The earliest documented history of New York includes the history of New Netherlands, the part of the New World controlled by Holland from 1609 until 1664 (when the English took control and New Netherlands became New York). It is understandable, then, that the first fuzzy accounts of metals and minerals involve the lower Hudson River corridor.

However, while my search for the oldest information about New York gold initially takes us a long way from the Blue Line, we remain well connected to the North Country. The birthplace of the Hudson, remember, is Lake Tear of the Clouds, on the south slope of Mount Marcy. John Mylod states, in *Biography of a River*, "… at a point 1,000 feet below the peak of Mount Marcy is Lake Tear of the Clouds, the beginning of one of the shortest and greatest runs to the sea. Lake Tear is part of a capillary network of creeks, small rivers, and streams that irrigate the Adirondack watershed and whose rushing waters combine to keep the Hudson running swiftly downhill to Troy."[1]

From Troy south the Hudson is a tidewater river, reversing flow at the commands of the sun and the moon. Because of its navigability to the Atlantic, the Hudson was plied by some very early explorers: its discoverer, Giovanno deVerrazano in 1524; Estevan Gomez in 1525; and numerous French fur traders throughout the 1500s.

Roland Zandt notes:

> Henry Hudson's voyage of 1609 gave us our first description of the river from its mouth to the head of navigation, and it provided the initial impetus for the first colonization of the Hudson valley. It is therefore appropriate that the river should bear his name.[2]

Adirondack prospector Millard Hayes, somewhere "northward of Bog River," meticulously inspects his gold pan for colors. *Warwick Carpenter, 2-11-1911*

Two of a prospecting party of five southbound on Tupper Lake in search of the source of a spectacular quartz-gold specimen. *"Lure of the Adirondack Gold," Warwick Carpenter, 2-11-1911*

It was as I was reading a mariner's log of Hudson's 1609 voyage that I came across some interesting entries about "Mynes" and "Metalls." The journal was kept by Robert Juet, probably a ship's officer, as one of his duties was to set the compass. He was aboard the *Half Moon* as skipper Henry Hudson took her gingerly up the Great River of the Mountains.

Selected entries from Juet's log:

September 5, 1609. This day many of the people came aboard, some in Mantles of Feathers, and some in Skinnes of divers sorts of good Furres. Some women also came to us with Hempe. They had red Copper tobacco pipes, and other things of Copper did they wear about their neckes.

September 12. This morning at our first rode in the River, there came eight and twenty Canoes full of men, women, and children to betray us, but we saw their intent, and suffered none of them to come aboard. At twelve of the clocke they departed. They brought with them oysters and Beanes, whereof we bought some. They have great tobacco pipes of yellow Copper...

September 30. This is a very pleasant place to build a Towne on. The Road is very neere, and very good for all winds, save an East-North-East wind. The Mountaynes looke as if some Metall or Mineral were in them, for the trees that grow on them were all blasted, and some of them barren with no Trees on them.

October 2. ... and hard by it there is a Cliffe, that looked the colour of a white greene, as though it were either a Copper or Silver Myne: and I think it to be one of them, by the Trees that grow upon it. For they be all burned, and other places are greene as Grasse.[3]

Juet's log entries are the earliest written source, which I have found, that allude to possible mineral/metal deposits in New York. The mention of "yellow Copper" is particularly intriguing. In fact, in a little book titled *The Lost Gold Mine Of The Hudson* (1915) author Tristram Coffin links a gold mine in "the River Hills" to the Indian descriptions which "excited the cupidity of Henrik Hudson and the crew of the *Half Moon*."[4]

Coffin narrates:

Indeed in the pages of authoritative history recorded after the death of Truman Hurd [Hurd and his faithful Indian companion, Uscung from Esopus, were supposed to have extracted huge quantities of gold from their mine], it is asserted that long before the discovery of the Shatumic [another native name for the Hudson] by the whites, the Indians knew

A threesome, all bitten by gold fever, scrutinize the offerings of a St. Lawrence County stream. *"Lure of the Adirondack Gold," Warwick Carpenter, 2-11-1911*

of a gold mine supposed to have been situated in the Shawangunk Mountains. Its precise location is said never to have been disclosed by them. In view of the facts and traditions connected with the subject, it was not surprising that many well-informed people came to believe that the now undoubted mine in the River Hills had been mistakenly asserted by the historians to have been located in the Shawangunk range.[5]

Fellow prospectors, at this point a bit of caution is in order, though degree of speculation, of course, is your call. An observant reader will notice that Coffin discreetly fashioned into the Dedication of his book a quasi-disclaimer. The story is described as a mixture of the historical and the traditional. And "traditional" may well be the author's intentionally cloudy term for "entirely fabricated." On the other hand, maybe there really is a lost gold mine somewhere along the Hudson.

As far as Juet's words are concerned, commentary from the good ship *Half Moon* about matters other than sailing and navigation are rendered less than rock solid by another description, this one of a mermaid:

> From the navel her back and breasts were like a woman's. Her skin was very white and long haire hanging down behind of colour blacke: in her going down they saw her tayle which was like the tayle of a porpoise and speckeled Macrell. The names that saw her were Thomas Hiles, and Robert Raynor. Written by myself, Henry Hudson.[6]

It appears that Hiles or Raynor or the ever-experimenting captain may have lit up some of that Hempe that came aboard with the colorful mantles of Feathers and lovely Skinnes of divers sorts of Furres.

Pure gold dreads not the fire

—Chinese Proverb

—3—

Ondessonk

Four decades after Robert Juet and Henry Hudson wrote about Minerals and Mynes and Mermaids, a Jesuit missionary sent detailed descriptions of the New World to his superiors in France. In one of those accounts he mentions a gold mine.

I have referred to this literary search for gold as a prospecting trek. As I was digging and sifting my way through the 2,800-page *The Documentary History of the State of New York*, I chanced upon the noblest kind of precious metal. The lode of which I speak lay, dross free, deep in the heart of a seventeenth-century Blackrobe. My life is the richer for having made the acquaintance of Father Jogues, a treasure of a man.

Isaac Jogues attended college and seminary amid the refined elegance of Renaissance France. Slight of build, he was a gentle, sensitive, compassionate man. In many ways it seemed that he was simply too tender, too sensitive for the rigors of a brutal, untamed land. Nevertheless, he joined the Society of Jesus (Jesuits), and in 1636 embarked as a missionary to the Huron Indians in Quebec, New France. He was given the name "Ondessonk," Huron for "bird of prey," an apt name, I have thought, for one whose eye was ever keen for men's hearts and whose spirit soared in the darkest of times.

In 1642, Father Jogues was captured by a war party of Mohawk Indians, avowed enemies of the French, and so of any French missionary, or Blackrobe. In the year of imprisonment that followed he was subjected to the most horrific torture. He was paraded from village to village all along the Mohawk River valley. At each location he was stripped naked and forced to stumble through a gauntlet of several hundred frenzied Mohawks as they poked and prodded and punched and kicked him.

At last, in July 1643, Father Jogues escaped from his Mohawk captors and made his way to the Dutch at Fort Orange (Albany). His stay in New Netherlands from 1642 to 1643 provided him with the details which he

"So now, we have in Father Jogues a 'reporter,' highly educated, skilled in discernment, fluent in Latin, French, Huron, and Iroquois, repulsed by rumors and superstition, straight talker even in the worst of times, who states [in a formal 1646 report to his mission superiors] that somewhere between the North River (Hudson) and the South River (Delaware), 'a gold mine is reported to have been found.' I figure his words are credible." Jogues death is memorialized by an evergreen cross laid out on a hillside overlooking the Mohawk River in Auriesville, where this statue is located.

later recorded at Three Rivers, New France, August 3, 1646.

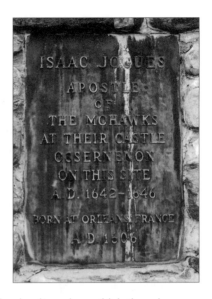

New Holland which the Dutch call in Latin *Novum Belgium*: in their own language Nieuw Nederland that is to say, New Low Countries, is situated between Virginia and New England. The mouth of the river called by some Nassau River [Hudson River] or the great North River (to distinguish it from another which they call the South river) and which in some maps that I have recently seen is also called, I think, River Maurice, is at 40 degrees, 30 minutes. Its channel is deep, fit for the largest ships that ascend to Man-hattes Island, which is seven leagues in circuit, and on which there is a fort to serve as the commencement of a town to be built there and to be called New Amsterdam [present day New York City]…

This country is bounded on the New England side by a river they call the *Fresche* river [Connecticut River], which serves as a boundary between them and the English. The English however come very near to

them rather than to be dependent on English Lords who would exact rents and would fain be absolute. On the other side southward toward Virginia, its limits are the river which they call the South river on which there is also a Dutch settlement, but the Swedes have at its mouth another [settlement] extremely well provided with men and cannon. It is believed that these Swedes are maintained by some merchants of Amsterdam, who are not satisfied that the West India Company should alone enjoy all the commerce of these parts. It is near this river [South] that a gold mine is reported to have been found.[1]

13

For Isaac Jogues, life's supreme wealth derived from loving and serving God. The search for gold, therefore, was not high on his priority list. He evidently chose to spend his life prospecting for the souls of men rather than for treasure which to him had no real value. He saw "riches" very differently than most of us. That, I suspect, is why gold is treated as an aside and is mentioned only in one sentence.

As I assay this priest's curious one-liner about a gold mine I am reminded that, unlike Juet and Hudson, Isaac Jogues had waged all out war against superstitious legends and fantastic tales. The crew of the *Half Moon,* it must be remembered, still believed that it was possible for a ship to fall off the horizon into a world inhabited by demons. It is apparent that Jogues, on the other hand, was a truth seeker, given to debunking far-fetched stories, not perpetuating them. The purpose of his writing was to provide no-nonsense, factual reports for the Jesuit mission agency. My sense is that Jogues must have been privy to substantive information for him to have included a gold mine in his account.

Near the end of his life Father Jogues, as French peace ambassador to the Iroquois, was accused by the Mohawks of being a wicked magician and of harboring a devil in a small black box, a box which actually held the priest's Mass equipment. The Iroquois had suffered a deadly epidemic and the Mohawks were convinced that Jogues and his "demon" box had caused their suffering. They announced their plans to kill him: "We will set your head on the points of the stockade, so that when we bring some of your brothers here captives, they may see you."[2]

Jogues was undaunted. Take note of his response: "I have no fear either of your torments or of death. I do not know why you threaten to kill me. I have come into your country to help you to preserve the peace, and to level the earth, and to show you the road to heaven. And you treat me like a dog. God governs the French and the Iroquois; He knows well how to punish you."[3]

Meek, tender-hearted Jogues unflinchingly rebukes his accusers even

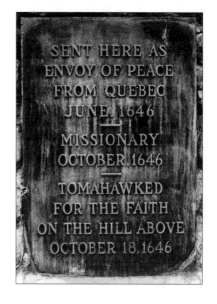

SENT HERE AS
ENVOY OF PEACE
FROM QUEBEC
JUNE 1646

MISSIONARY
OCTOBER 1646

TOMAHAWKED
FOR THE FAITH
ON THE HILL ABOVE
OCTOBER 18 1646

as he faces death. His composure and his penetrating, scolding words bear witness that uncompromised straight talk was another characteristic of his.

So now, we have in Father Jogues a "reporter," highly educated, skilled in discernment, fluent in Latin, French, Huron, and Iroquois, repulsed by rumors and superstition, straight-talker even in the worst of situations, who states that somewhere between the North River [Hudson] and the South River (Delaware) "a gold mine is reported to have been found." I figure his words are credible. And I guess here is as good a place as any to note that through the years there have been numerous accounts of downstate gold mines, several of them investigated by George Heusser in *Gold, Silver, and Other Mines of the Shawangunks*.[4]

Two months after Father Jogues, with grotesquely crippled hands, wrote his description of New Netherlands, his skull was split by a Mohawk hatchet. He was decapitated and, just as his captors had threatened, his head was placed on a tall stake of the village fence.

Shortly before his murder he wrote a colleague in France about his decision to become peace envoy to the Iroquois: "And so if I be employed in this mission, my heart tells me, '*Ibo et non redibo*—I shall go but I shall not return'"[5] Later in the same letter Isaac tells why he must go back to the very ones who had hated and tortured him: "In conclusion, that Iroquois people is the spouse of blood to me; this people have I espoused to me with my blood."[6]

I have traveled the Thruway a hundred times since I first made the trip in 1964 from Skowhegan, Maine to Houghton College, in western New York. A hundred times I have passed by an evergreen cross laid out on the side of a hill overlooking the Mohawk River. I know now that the Auriesville Shrine marks the place where Father Isaac Jogues died at the hands of those whom he loved beyond words and to whom he felt espoused.

And now, when I drive by that hillside cross, ever green, I am reminded of a priest's passing comment about a gold mine. But the green cross also reminds me of Mohawk Valley's first European settlers, of the indigenous Iroquois, of the valiant Blackrobes, and how these intertwining seventeenth-century lives were affected by both the laser light of authentic compassion and the entombing darkness of superstition and greed. I am reminded, too, of the quality of treasure, noble or ignoble, shining or cankered, illusory or eternal, that may lie in the hearts of men.

A poignant proof of what gold does to the human soul was found in the rubble of Pompeii—a petrified corpse still clutching a bag of gold after seventeen centuries, one possession the man would not leave behind when he fled in panic, only to be caught, asphyxiated, and entombed, by the volcano Vesuvius.

Gold: An Illustrated History
—Vincent Buranelli

—4—

Fort Orange and the Deep Sea

In 1841, Judge Jeremiah Johnson of Brooklyn translated into English a 1659 Dutch manuscript, "A Description Of The New Netherlands." The actual author, Adriaen Van der Donck, served as a kind of seventeenth-century district attorney to the fledgling colony of Renssalaerwyck (now the Rensselaer and Albany areas) from 1641 to 1655. In fact, as he had obtained his Doctorate of Laws degree in Holland, this fellow is very likely the first lawyer in New York's history.

In his account Van der Donck tells how he personally witnessed an assay performed on a specimen believed to be New Netherlands gold. Discussing the "minerals, earths and stones" found in the Dutch part of the New World, he states:

> Considering that the Netherlanders are not numerous in the country, the discovery of minerals of more value than iron would attract the attentions and cupidity of powerful and jealous friends, who in time might easily oust us, and shut the door against us, and then occupy and rule in our possessions. Passing by such speculative probabilities, and to satisfy the inquiries of our real friends, we will describe more particularly some facts and occurrences which have passed at several places, on the subject of minerals. It is now placed beyond doubt that valuable minerals abound in the country, as experiments and satisfactory proofs have been made to establish those facts by the direction of Governor Kieft, in several instances, as well of gold as of quicksilver.[1]

Compared to my literary encounter with Isaac Jogues, learning about William Kieft was like digging up some kind of toxic anti-treasure. Kieft, Director General (Governor) of New Netherlands from 1638 to 1647, became furious with the Wappinger Indians of the lower Hudson for their refusal to pay a freshly levied tax. He decided in February of 1643 to "wipe the mouths of the Indians." In other words, he would teach them a

17

lesson they would not forget. I have included excerpts of this grisly matter lest for one moment you think that grotesque evil was peculiar to Mohawk Indians.

One night Kieft sent out a detachment of Dutch soldiers with the express purpose of slaughtering a number of Indian refugees who had fled to the Fort Amsterdam (New York City) area to escape a Mohawk war party. The notes of David de Vries, 1655, describe the debacle:

> When it was day the soldiers returned to the fort [Fort Orange, today's Albany] having massacred or murdered eighty Indians and considering they had done a deed of Roman valor, in murdering so many in their sleep: where infants were torn from their mother's breasts, and hacked to pieces in the presence of parents, and the pieces thrown into the fire and the water, and other sucklings, being bound to small boards were cut, stuck, and pierced, and miserably massacred in a manner to move a heart of stone.... This is a disgrace to our nation, who have so generous a governor in our Fatherland as the Prince of Orange, who has always endeavored in his wars to spill as little blood as possible.[2]

The resulting bitter and bloody war between the New Netherlands colonists and the Indians (including the Mohawks) lasted until 1645. It was then that peace negotiations began at Rensselaerwyck. These talks are the setting for Van der Donck's account of what I believe are the first documented "tests for gold" in New York:

> To proceed with the treaty, the citizens of Rensselaerwyck procured a certain Indian, named Agheroense, to attend and serve as interpreter, who was well known to the Christians, having been much among them, and who spoke and understood all the Indian languages which were spoken by the parties that attended the negotiations. As the Indians are generally disposed to paint and ornament their faces with several brilliant colours, it happened on a certain morning that this Indian interpreter, who lodged at the Director's house, came down stairs, and in the presence of the Director and myself sat down, and began stroking and painting his face. The Director observed the operation, and requested me to inquire of the Indian what substance he was using, which he handed to me, and I passed it to the Director, who examined the same attentively, and judged from its weight and from its greasy and shining appearance that the lump contained some valuable metal, for which I commuted with the Indian, to ascertain what it contained. We acted with it according to the best of

our judgement, and gave the same to be proved by a skilful doctor of medicine, named Johannes La Montagne, of the Council in the New Netherlands. The lump of mineral was put into a crucible, which was placed in a fire, and after the same had according to my opinion, been in the fire long enough, it was taken out, when it delivered two pieces of gold worth about three guilders.[3]

The gold experiments of Governor Kieft are also reported in a 1671 Dutch document by Arnoldus Montanus. This account establishes that the Indian interpreter actually pointed toward the mountain which was the source of his golden face paint.[4]

However, there are no mountains actually observable from the site of Fort Orange, which was located on the west bank of the Hudson at river level. The nearest visible high ground would have been the elevated terrain on the east side of the Hudson or the rise which ascends westerly from the river and upon which Albany's Empire Plaza is perched. Nevertheless, the Montanus report allows you to reasonably speculate that Agheroense's "gold" was not that far from Fort Orange. He could have pointed toward the Adirondacks. (Maybe he was pointing to the Taconics. If so, here's an interesting note: one of the most macabre murders ever committed in New York was supposed to have involved a gold mine located in the Taconic Mountains, right on the New York-Massachusetts border. Patricia Edwards Clyne provides the gruesome details in "The Cannibal of Columbia County.")[5]

Efforts to verify Kieft's assay result were mysteriously doomed. An English ship, captained by George Lamberton, left the port of New Haven in 1646.[6] On board were samples of the Fort Orange gold and a Kieft-appointed guardian, Arent Corson.[7] Though historians have been unable to name the ship, they know she set sail for England in January, "foundered at sea, and was never heard from again."[8]

Never heard from again, that is, until a ghost ship fitting her description appeared one day off New Haven. Cotton Mather tells of this apparition in his *Magnalia Cristi Americana*,[9] and Henry Wadsworth Longfellow commemorates the eerie event in a poem called "The Phantom Ship." A few stanzas follow:

And at last their prayers were answered:
    It was the month of June,
An hour before the sunset
    Of a windy afternoon,

When steadily steering landward,
    A ship was seen below,
And they knew it was Lamberton, Master,
    Who sailed so long ago.

On she came with a cloud of canvas,
    Right against the wind that blew
Until the eye could distinguish
    The faces of the crew.

Then fell her straining topmasts,
    Hanging tangled in the shrouds,
And her sails were loosened and lifted,
    And blown away like clouds.

And the masts, with all their rigging,
    Fell slowly, one by one,
And the hulk dilated and vanished,
    As a sea-mist in the Sun!

And the people who saw this marvel
    Each said unto his friend,
That this was the mould of their vessel,
    And thus her tragic end.

And the pastor of the village
    Gave thanks to God in prayer,
That, to quiet their troubled spirits,
    He had sent this Ship of Air.[10]

No less determined by the loss of the Lamberton ship, Kieft would send a second collection of the Fort Orange gold samples to Holland. This time he, himself, would guard the special cargo. As fate would have it, the second ship, the *Princess,* was also lost at sea, off the Welsh coast in September

1647.[11] A Dutch letter dated October 13, 1649, reported that the *Princess* had contained "a hundred samples of minerals" and "exact maps." [12]

Maps, samples, and a particularly disgraceful colonial governor—enriched, sadly, with the corrosive, anti-precious metals of arrogance and cruelty—were all confiscated by the ocean depths.

And the sea, of course, would never relinquish them.

Good morning to the day, and next, my gold!

Volpone
—Ben Johson

—5—

Soft Gold and Sea Shells

"Got colors!" is your happy yell, gold pan in your hands, at the final stages of your meticulous dipping and swirling and rinsing and sifting. Colors are those heavy, auriferous particles that have resisted the centrifuge effect of your gyrating hands. There the golden grains lie, on the business surface of your pan, teased out into the sunlight and now smiling up at you. What might the next scoop yield?

In my prospecting quest for literary references about native New York gold I panned quite a bit in the streams and tributaries of history between the mid-seventeenth and mid-eighteenth centuries, but I simply didn't get any decent colors. There are, I think, four reasons.

First, seventeenth-century North Country prospectors, and all other prospectors who have ever tried a hand at romancing the stones, bow before a sobering geological truism: for the most part, this planet's gold lies in distributions that are invisible and inaccessible. That, obviously, is why gold is a "rare" precious metal.

Second, it's one thing to go prospecting in a period of history where there is a semblance of social tranquility. It is quite another thing to jaunt starry-eyed through the wilderness looking for gold when, whether you're Indian or European, there is likely a hefty reward for your top knot. Prospecting and getting scalped resonate poorly.

Third, the overwhelming ruggedness of the Adirondacks discouraged many would-be prospectors. Throughout the Yukon gold rush of 1898, Northwest Mounted Police were stationed all over the Klondike trails and in the mining camps. In the seventeenth-century and eighteenth-century North Country, by contrast, you were on your own. Tharrett Gilbert Best comments: "One map drawn in 1756 states that the region, because of its mountains and 'drowned lands,' was impassable and uninhabitable."[1] And Theobold Clark notes: "Grim and forbidding, the Great Wilderness remained

23

so long inhospitable that even in 1776, on Governor Pownal's map of New York, the following inscription covered the whole area: This vast Tract of Land which is the Ancient Couchsachrage, one of the Four Beaver Hunting Countries of the Six nations, is not yet surveyed."[2]

Fourth, and perhaps most significantly, New Netherlands and the first New Yorkers had already discovered "soft gold," beaver fur, in enormous quantities and readily marketable. The all-pervasive fur trade was so economically central to colonial lifestyle that conventional European currency and coinage was completely replaced with a monetary system tied solely to beaver pelts, barter goods, and wampum. According to Gilbert Hagerty, "The beaver as a commodity of exchange in New Netherlands became so important that it was represented on the official seal of the colony. Frequently business was transacted, debts paid, and services exchanged in terms of beavers. Beaver skins were the surest pay in New Netherlands, not only in 1657, when this was observed, but during the entire period of Dutch settlement."[3]

Wampum consisted of beads made from sea shells. Quahog clam shells, the best of them found on the fine sands of Long Island's Hempstead Bay, were the source of both white and purple beads. The Indians worked bits of shell into tiny tubules that were then strung into bracelets, necklaces, belts, and funeral ornaments. Referring to the St. Lawrence Indians, Father Paul La Juene described wampum as "their gold and silver, their diamonds and their pearls."[4] Peter Kalm, in the 1760s, commented, "a traveler, well-stocked with wampum beads, may become a considerable gainer in trade with the Indians, but if he takes gold or bullion, he will undoubtedly be a loser. The Indians put little or no value on metals."[5]

At this point you are likely thinking, "Dude, we've been goldhounding for a while and all we have so far are a few glittering flecks from North Lake, yellow metal tobacco pipes, a bedazzling mermaid with a 'speckeled Macrell tayle,' beatifically golden character traits of a French Blackrobe, that missionary's mention of a gold mine, and nasty Governor Kieft's shipwrecked gold. Now we add beaver hides and clams. When are we going to hit some pay dirt?"

Hang on to your pans, fellow prospectors. We're about to hit on some colors. Thanks, in a circuitous kind of way, to Dingle Dangle Jones.

Gold is the most cowardly and treacherous of all metals. It makes no treaty that it does not break. It has no friend whom it does not sooner or later destroy.

—U.S. Senator John Ingalls
45th Congress

—6—

Public Lands Law and Dingle Dangle Jones

The English, because of the discoveries of John Cabot in 1497, never really recognized the Dutch ownership of New Netherlands. In 1664, Charles II of England decided to "give" New Netherlands to his brother James, Duke of York and Albany. To execute this gift-giving affair, Colonel Richard Nicolls, with a fleet of four ships and 400 men, sailed into New Amsterdam harbor with a splendid show of force. A few blood-less days later New Netherlands became New York and Fort Orange became Albany.

There followed the French and Indian War and, in 1775, the beginning of the American Revolution. While en route to Kingston, the Provincial Congress of New York met at White Plains and authorized delegates at Philadelphia to sign the Declaration of Independence. Willis Fletcher Johnstone notes: "The next day, July 10, 1776, the Provincial Congress changed its own political title to that of 'Convention of Representatives of the STATE OF NEW YORK.' The Empire State was born."[1]

With exuberant sovereignty New York took title to all tracts of land formerly held by the Crown. To perpetuate settlement the infant state anx-iously began to sell off its new holding by issuing Letters Patent. There was a catch to these documents, a huge catch for prospectors. No Letters Patent could be issued absent a clear explanation that any discovered deposits of gold or silver belonged to the State.

I would very much like to report to you that with passing years the State became less possessive. That is not, however, the case. From the ear-liest Letters Patent to the most current statutes, New York has always held sole title to deposits of gold within its borders.[2] Whether I find gold on the Forest Preserve or in my own flower garden, it belongs to the State.

I probably never would have made this unhappy discovery if it hadn't

27

been for Dingle Dangle Jones. There are some things we know and some things we don't know about Dingle Dangle. We know he was real. Mrs. Mooney, Forestport librarian, personally knew his grandson.[3] And Howard Thomas established that Dingle Dangle was once postmaster of Steuben Valley and belonged to a debating club in Floyd. Like Atwell Martin (after whom the little settlement at North Lake is named) and other North Country hermits, a disastrous romance had sent Dingle Dangle into the Adirondacks, where hunting, fishing, and trapping might take his mind off a broken heart.[4] We also know that Dingle Dangle claimed to have discovered gold:

> Back in 1894, Dingle Dangle took a prospecting trip to Ice Cave Mountain at the northern end of North Lake and came back with gold. He told friends that he sent samples down to Newark, New Jersey, for assay

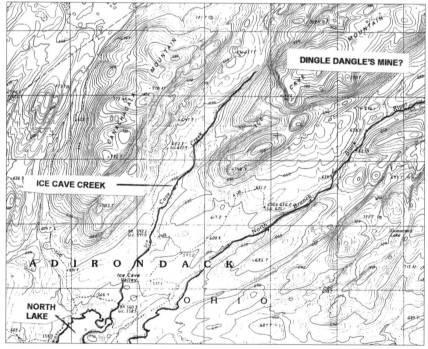

Both Ice Cave Creek and the North Branch of the Black River surely become natural mineral sluices during spring run-off. Finding color-bearing sand or gold-flecked quartz in either location might offer a clue about the legendary gold mine of the hermit Dingle Dangle Jones. *Map courtesy of U.S. Geological Survey (Honnedaga Lake Quadrangle)*

but the experts had written that the lode would produce only twelve dollars a ton and was not worth working. Folks who saw his samples claimed that the gold was mixed with silver, but Dingle Dangle never let on that he had discovered anything but pure gold.[5]

What we don't know about Dingle Dangle is what happened to him. Thomas said Jones was last seen by some guides at the Adirondack League Club's Forest Lodge on Honnedaga Lake. Apparently Dingle Dangle started off into the woods for his camp. That was the last anyone ever saw him. In utter mystery he became part of the ancient beaver hunting grounds of the Iroquois. Neither do we know about the veracity of Dingle Dangle's find or of his assay results.

Dingle Dangle Jones may have panned the North Branch of the Black River. The question is, how much would the state know about his auriferous exploits?

It was, nevertheless, the Thomas account of Dingle Dangle's "gold" that had reminded me of my own discovery at Ice Cave Creek and had inspired me to call Dr. Kelly. In that phone conversation, to which I have already alluded, the State Mineralogist told me about a "gold file" in his office and recommended that I come to Albany and look it over.

Then he told me about the museum's two official specimens of Adirondack gold, one from the Sacandaga River area and the other from the Moose River area. Both samples were "placer" gold, he said, gold that via weather and erosion got "placed" some distance from the source.

In a follow-up to our phone conversation, Dr. Kelly sent me several print-outs, one of which was a photocopy of current Public Lands Law. Below is an excerpt:

Section 81. Minerals subject to state ownership:

1. The following minerals are the property of the people of New York in their right of sovereignty:

(a) All deposits of gold and silver in or upon private lands and lands belonging to the state heretofore or hereafter discovered within this state.[6]

There follows in the Public Lands Law a giant Pandora's Box regarding deposits of gold and silver. The state is less greedy than it first seems. According to the law, while a citizen can never actually own gold or silver, he may file a Notice of Discovery with the Secretary of State, and eventually be allowed to benefit from the mining of his find.

Section 82. Notice of discovery; filing fee; bounty to discover; royalty to state.

1. Any person discovering a mine or deposit of gold or silver in or upon private lands within this state and any mineral in or upon state lands may work the same subject to the provision of this article but not until he files written notice of such discovery with the secretary of state, which notice shall be indexed and registered in a permanent record to be kept by such secretary, describing particularly the nature and situation of such mine or minerals.

2. Notices filed pursuant to this section shall be in such form as the secretary of state shall prescribe and shall contain, among other things, the following:
   (a) the name and the address of the filer
   (b) the name and owner of the land
   (c) an accurate description together with a map made on tracing cloth with India ink of the land against which the notice is filed, in form sufficient for the convenient location of the land, which land shall, so far as practicable be of equal length and width and shall comprise not more than forty acres.
   (d) a statement subscribed by the filer and affirmed by him to be true under the penalties of perjury that he has read and knows the provisions of this article and is familiar with the conditions to be by him performed precedent to the acquisition, continuation, and preservation of any rights flowing from his filing of such notice.

3. A fee of fifty dollars shall be paid to the secretary of state with each notice.[7]

Section 82 goes on to explain that the filer shall have sole benefit of minerals extracted so long as a royalty is paid to the State (and as long as the find is not on Forest Preserve lands). This Notice of Discovery procedure has been around, in some format, for a long time. Between December 1791 and December 1997, over 11,000 *sworn statements* about discoveries of gold and silver have been filed in the Office of the Secretary of State![8]

Next to a vehicle barrier this lettered rock block points the way to Ice Cave Mountain. Dingle Dangle may have tramped the same trail to his alleged secret gold mine.

There's a fair chance that wherever you've tramped or canoed in the Adirondacks, the ground beneath your feet and the stream/lake bed beneath your hull was claimed by someone, at some time, to have been gold-bearing.

Gold and love affairs are hard to hide.

—Spanish Proverb

—7—

Archives and Sandwich Bags

In November 1997, I finally got to do some prospecting down in Albany, at the Cultural Education Center. Many of us know this building as the State Museum, occasional Jurassic parking place for "Dinosaurs Alive." I realized that, given the New York State Public Lands Law and its statutory predecessors, a big part of the search for gold in the Adirondacks must be a matter of public record. The task, therefore, was to track down the Notices of Discovery required by law to be filed with the Secretary of State for each gold "discovery." I eventually found them, ten floors above the museum's main exhibit halls.

In 1971, per the Legislature, the State Archives were created within the State Education Department and were to be part of the "memory bank of the State's culture." In the eleventh floor cloistered sanctuary of the rare and the crumbling, I found thirteen archive cases containing twenty-three huge, leather-bound volumes, each titled *Register of New York Gold and Silver Mines*. By the way, visiting the Archives is a lot like visiting an inmate in a maximum security prison. You leave all personal items in lockers outside the research room, produce iron-clad identification, and read through a list of twenty-plus strictly observed rules. Then you go to the main desk and sign the research log. As you're writing you hear the main entry doors electronically lock behind you. With the ominous, magnetic clicking of the dead bolts you become one with forever-incarcerated printed things—genealogical records, colonial maps, lots and lots of very old books.

The guards, that is, the archivists, graciously allowed me to bring in a miniature tape recorder so that I could whisper various excerpts onto tape instead of penciling notes (pens and notebooks are aggressively prohibited). Unfortunately, instead of bringing along a blank tape, I had somehow inserted a golden oldies tape. As I was not exactly proficient with this newly purchased recorder, and because I was wearing white,

Museum-issue cotton gloves that I could only get half on, the sounds of solemn, archival silence were every now and then interrupted with spurts of "Come On Baby Light My Fire" and "Jeremiah Was A Bullfrog."

At each of these ever-so-brief accidents I wanted very much to raise my hands and proclaim to the startled authorities, "Hey, it's not entirely my fault. See for yourselves. The gloves don't fit!" But I didn't. And amazingly, I was not ejected from New York State's venerable memory bank of culture. Rather, I was actually able to browse all twenty-three volumes, "golden" oldies in their own right.

On the first page of Book One I found this heading in longhand: "Abstract of the Descriptions of Gold and Silver Mines Recorded in the Deed Books in the Secretary's Office." The first entry on that page is by Beriah Palmer, who claimed that in the "County of Saratoga, Town of Half Moon, 100 rods below Cohoes Falls there is both gold and silver ore." The entry is dated December 19, 1791. There follow literally thousands of Notices of Discovery, every one of them a sworn statement! And yes, gold is claimed to have been found in every single county of the Adirondack Park. As evidence of Klondike gold fever igniting in New York, there are six volumes, representing four or five thousand Adirondack claims, for 1898 alone!

A typical entry, this one about a site not all that far from Dingle Dangle Jones' discovery, reads as follows:

> To the Secretary of the State of New York, Notice is hereby given that the subscribers have discovered a mine of Gold and Silver and tributaries

Three registers of gold mines in the state archives.

Folder No. 29 of "Mining Claims, Filed pursuant to section 82, Article 7 of the Public Lands Law, 1985-1990," bulges with gold mine claims and sandwich bags of actual ore.

situated in the County of Herkimer, State of New York, in Township #1 on Moose River Tract on the inlet of Nelson Lake. This notice given in pursuance of the statutes of this State in such case made and provide. Dated Port Leyden, September 8, 1879. John Schroeder and G. Hoage. Filed and Recorded September 9, 1879 and agrees with the original as compared therewith by me, Geo. Moss, Deputy Secretary of State.

Another entry:

Notice of Discovery of a Mine
To the Secretary of the State of New York

Please take notice that the undersigned citizen of the State of New York has discovered a valuable mine of gold and silver in the nature of a placer mine including all the soil, gravel, rock and other mineral substances bearing gold and silver, located on, over, and beneath the surface of the earth within the boundary line of a certain Lot Number 11, Region 3, of Township #1 of John Brown's Tract of Macomb's Purchase, partly in the Town of Lyonsdale, County of Lewis, State of New York, and partly in the Town of Webb, County of Herkimer, in said State, according to the boundaries and numbers shown on the Adirondack Map published by the Forestry, Fish, and Game Commission in 1908, the location to be known as the Lyonsdale #9 Mine. As to the discovery of said mine the undersigned hereby claims all the bounties, rights, benefits, and privileges conferred by the laws for himself, his heirs, executors, administrators, and assigns, and requests proper registry thereof this 7th day of August 1911.

The phrase "on, over, and beneath the surface of the earth" is as curious as it is comprehensive. Just what kind of mineral deposits are found "over" the earth's surface? Auriferous cloud formations? Or maybe lunar lode, as when a moon mine gets poised exactly over Lot #11 in John Brown's Tract?

A few years back Elizabeth Folwell, Editor-at-Large for *Adirondack Life*, must have also done some prospecting at the State Archives. She discovered this interesting claim, dated July 30, 1881, and penned by a Richard Rosa:

> ...I hereby give notice that I have discovered a mine of gold and silver in the county of Hamilton.... The metal is found in large lumps free from quartz or other worthless matter. The Lumps very in size from a quarter cup to a bushel basket. Location: the bottom of the central portion of Lake Pleasant in the Town of Lake Pleasant. The lead commences a that point and thence perpendicularly until it strikes the upper confines of China.[1]

While the gold and silver mine books in the Archives are accessed a dozen or so times a year, there are other claims that are rarely viewed, though they are as public as the Archive Registers. These are the most recent Notices of Discovery, and I found them in a Department of State office complex located at 41 State Street, Albany. There, somewhere on the third floor, is a brown, expandable document envelope titled, "Mining Claims, Misc. Papers, Folder No. 29." I was able to examine the packet, apparently never before requested, in the "customer service area" for New York State Corporations, on the second floor. The bulging folder was retrieved by a corporation specialist who had been pressed into service for an assignment that was not, I'm sure, part of his job description. He was instructed to be my "gold claims monitor." His specific orders were to stand by my side and watch my every move. I untied the string around the envelop and slid out a three-inch-high stack of dog-eared papers. On the top there was a cover page with the accompanying notation: "Filed pursuant to section 82, Article 7 of the Public Lands Law." Beneath this page there was a list of forty claims, filed between 1985 and 1990.

Exact descriptions accompanied each Notice of Discovery, along with official receipts for the required filing fees. Two individuals claiming they discovered gold in Warren County filed multiple claims, costing nearly $500 per claimant! Most intriguing were several sandwich bags full of actual gold-looking samples. When I slid these out the corporation specialist became wide-eyed with excitement. In an instant I knew what happened. He had caught a bit of gold fever, right before my eyes. In addition to the bagged "ore," I discovered a very authentic-looking certificate of assay of a sample taken from Macomb's Purchase which stated that testing by fire (reminiscent of Van Kieft's tests at Fort Orange) yielded both gold and silver.

When I finished looking through Folder 29, a question formed in my mind: Did Dr. Kelly know about the State Street sandwich bags?

He did not, I would learn when I stopped by his office for a visit and a long look at his gold file.

In relatively pure form gold has unrivaled qualities of malleability and ductility. One troy ounce of gold, for example, can be drawn into a hair-like thread fifty miles long. The same amount of gold, no larger than a sugar lump, coats more than a thousand miles of silver or copper wire.... One troy ounce can be beaten to a golden film so thin that one thousand sheets would be needed to make up the thickness of this page. A three-inch cube can be made into a sheet covering an acre.

The Magic of Gold
—Jenifer Marx

—8—

The Gold File

On February 13, 1998, I met Dr. William Kelly in his office on the third floor of the State Museum in Albany. Dr. Kelly, whose actual title at the time was State Curator of Minerals, is a leading authority on New York State mining and quarry history. He is also, of course, an expert at mineral identification. I sensed immediately that I was in a place where romancing the stones was pursued with the fervor of an adolescent's first love.

Dr. Kelly guided me down cavernous aisles walled to the ceiling with racks of heavy-duty steel shelving. Upon the shelves lay ten thousand specimens from every corner of the state. All around me, I realized, was the geological history of New York, as written in rock and collected, chiseled, caressed, and scrutinized through the decades by ever-inquiring paramours of the earth's crust.

Dr. Kelly then showed me the Museum's two gold specimens, tiny in size, but authentic placer, and verifiably retrieved from the North Country. I also looked at Adirondack samples of fool's gold: mica, pyrite, and chalcopyrite. The mica sure resembled the flecks I'd found at North Lake.

We moved around some chunks of what looked like quartz and uncovered the surface of a desk, and there I sat, surrounded by rocks, browsing Dr. Kelly's "gold file." The folder contained newspaper clippings, magazine articles, and various gold-related papers written by Museum staff over the years.

For us North Country wannabe prospectors, some of this material is disheartening, but other commentary is exciting and downright fever-inducing. Annotations and excerpts of some of the gold file enclosures follow:

The Sacandaga Mining and Milling Co.
and the 'Sutphen Process'

In 1898, J. N. Nevius reports to the New York State Museum Director on an investigation of the Sacandaga Mining and Milling Co., located on the north bank of the Sacandaga River, west of Hadley, Saratoga County.

According to Nevius, William T. Bullis discovered gold in the sands of the Glens Falls area in 1883, and, "About the same time, Dr. C.P. Bellows, a dentist from Gloversville, collected a sample of black sand from a neighboring stream and had it assayed. The report stated the value to be $7.63 a ton. Bellows undertook an investigation and arrived at conclusions similar to those of Mr. Bullis. Other investigators were C.O. Yale, inventor of the famous lock, and Alonzo Chase of Redfield, S.D. The latter made a great many tests of sands from Hamilton and Fulton Counties, and states that the average value obtained was $4 a ton."

Nevius says that John E. Sutphen of Albany "took up the investigation with Mr. Bullis. After the death of the latter, Mr. Sutphen developed the process which bears his name and which is being tried for the first time on a commercial scale at this mill."

A detailed description is given of the gold mill and the chemistry of the Sutphen process. Alleged results from trial runs were from $5.40 to $7.40 a ton. A mill superintendent is cited as stating that 100 tons of sand produced $530 worth of gold at an expense of $2.50 a ton.

Nevius then states that samples of Hadley sand were tested for the Museum, not by the Sutphen Process but by the usual fire assay. The results obtained showed only trace values of gold. The universally accepted accuracy of the fire assay is affirmed, and the Sutphen Process is found by Nevius to be most dubious.[1]

"Memoranda As To Discovery of Mines of Gold and Silver"

This 1902 memoranda is directed to the general public and explains that "New York does not make any assay of gold or silver discovered, and therefore, whenever the discoverer desires any assay or analysis of any ore, etc., to be made, he must procure it to be made at his own expense."

It is further stated in this two-page document that, "The Secretary of State furnishes no blank forms of notice of discovery, but a good form of notice is appended hereto, which can be adapted in each particular case."

This sample Notice of Discovery is as follows:

Port Henry, N.Y., January 1, 1902
To the Secretary of State,

PLEASE TAKE NOTICE. That the undersigned has discovered a mine of gold and silver, in the Town of Moriah, County of Essex, and State aforesaid, situated upon Lot number three hundred and seventy-one, in the Paradox Tract, in said town, upon the farm now operated by John Johnson. Said mine is found in rock and gravel deposit upon said farm, and the vein or lead thereof runs in a northerly and southerly direction across the west end of said farm, and was discovered by me June 30,1901, and is more particularly described as follows:* Beginning about twenty rods east from the southwest corner of said lot, in a small brook known as Trout Brook, thence following the said brook, in a northerly direction, covering a strip of land fifteen rods in width on each side thereof, across the farm of John Johnson, a distance one hundred rods.

The undersigned hereby claims said mine, and all rights, benefits and privileges as discoverer thereof, given him by the statute in such case made and provided.

John Smith

(A verification may be added here, if desired.)
*In case the discoverer has a description of his mining claim, by metes and bounds, he can insert the same here.[2]

"Gold in the Adirondacks"

This 1910 article includes a letter by B. J. Hatmaker of Lowville, New York, dated January 19, 1910. Hatmaker states: "I have made upward of 200 fire assays of sand from Lewis County during the last few months. About half of these assays gave from $1 to $4 dollars per ton. Some large deposits averaged about $3."

It is further reported that Hatmaker sent samples of his gold-bearing alluvial sand to *The Engineering And Mining Journal*, which, in turn, had assays performed by two separate, reputable firms. Their tests indicated the presence of gold at only ten cents per ton.[3]

Gold Found on St. Lawrence County Farm

In 1922, the *Ogdensburg Journal* reported the following:

> Nestled in the foothills of the Adirondacks, about five miles from
> the village of Edwards, over some of the worst roads that exist in this
> section of New York State, is the farm of Ward Stammer, 75-year-old
> veteran of the Klondike rush, whose 400 acres in St. Lawrence County
> have now become famous because of the discovery of large quantities
> of gold abounding in the sands of all parts of the property…
> That gold is to be had in several sections near Edwards, Fullerville,
> Fine, and other places that rest in the neighborhood of the Adirondacks,
> has been known to chemists for a number of years, but a successful
> process for separating the gold from the sand has held up the mining
> industry in that region because it was believed unprofitable because of
> the large expenses of the separation.[4]

"The Prospect of Gold Discoveries in New York State"

In this 1933, Museum publication also known as "Circular 12," State
Geologist D.H. Newland reports on investigations of Adirondack gold
sands near Hadley, Saratoga County and along the Black River in Lewis
County. He concludes that gold occurs in those sands at only trace levels.
Newland notes:

> The Adirondacks are a southward extension of the Canadian Shield,
> that vast area (2,000,000 square miles) of Precambrian rocks which
> encircles Hudson Bay and extends to the Arctic Ocean on the north and
> the coasts of Labrador and Newfoundland on the northeast. Parts of this
> area are well mineralized. Gold, copper, nickel, and silver are produced
> by Canada on a liberal scale. There is thus an apparent basis for the idea
> frequently expressed that similar mineral deposits should be present
> south of the Canadian line. Broad generalizations of the kind have little
> basis in fact, however; the mineralized districts of Canada are found
> within geological formations and under sets of conditions not known to
> be duplicated in our own State.

Newland does admit, though, that gold may "yet be found in small
stringers of quartz in free condition, or it may be held in combination with
the sulphides of other metals, particularly those of iron and copper, which

are encountered here and there among the older rocks."

Included in Circular 12 is a discussion of alleged gold bearing sand in Cherry Valley. That sand, too, according to Newland, contains only trace amounts of gold. The report's conclusion contains a warning about auriferous sand enterprises: "The total outlay thus involved, for which no return has been forthcoming, probably amounts to hundreds of thousands of dollars."[5]

"Golden Dreams"

James Davis, New York State Geologist until 1979, authored this undated (though probably written in the 70s) informal, newsletter-type article. After presenting a brief account of Van der Donck's description of New Netherland gold, Davis said, "In many ways it is almost dangerous to reprint such accounts because many citizens may be tempted to grab picnic lunches and picks and charge over the landscape in search of 'Mohawk millions.'"

Three elements common to most tales of golden treasure are discussed: (1) the alleged find is identified by unqualified persons, (2) misfortune derails a venture before scientific verification, (3) the find is made during a time in which successful gold recovery is made elsewhere. After citing several examples of gold swindles, Davis concluded, "The search for gold in New York has been more successful in the pockets of the gullible than in the depths of the earth."[6]

"Thar Still Is Gold In Them Thar Hills"

Jim McGuire's 1984 *Schenectady Gazette* piece is about placer gold panned by Fulton County's deputy historian, Lewis Decker. McGuire writes, "People in these parts have mostly forgotten the fact that there's a bit o' gold to be found in the Adirondacks."

Decker and his wife apparently took a few lessons in panning and set out for an undisclosed streambed. In a few hours they "got colors," and later forwarded their find to State Mineralogist William Kelly. A letter to the Deckers from Dr. Kelly is quoted:

> The specimens you have brought in are quite angular, indicating that
> they have not traveled a great distance from their source area, at least not

by being water carried. The bedrock in the area from which the sample came is metamorphosed sedimentary and volcanic rock. In any event, this occurrence of gold raises some interesting geologic questions.[7]

Decker's gold was one of the two New York specimens which Dr. Kelly showed me on February 13, 1998.

"Gold in New York State"

Writing for *Gold Prospector* in 1987, Andy Maslowski states:

> All of the gold found in New York has been located within the Adirondack Mountains in the northern part of the state. These mountains are among the oldest in the world and have exhibited positive relief throughout much of the geologic period. Crystalline rocks within this province do contain gold-bearing quartz veins, but up to the present, all mining ventures have been unable to find commercial reserves.

Maslowski mentions that several gold mines in St. Lawrence and Franklin Counties were operated in the 1880s, but that the cost of extraction and processing was always greater than the value of recovered gold.

The New York State Department of Environmental Conservation, Division of Mineral Resources, has confirmed, according to Maslowski, that small gold finds, recovered by placer mining have occurred in the tributaries of the St. Regis and Saranac Rivers in the Adirondacks. The article concludes:

> Small amounts of placer gold continue to be located in the state, and the crystalline rocks of the Adirondack and Catskill Mountains offer huge targets for future gold exploration if and when the first major gold strike is ever made.[8]

Panning for gold in the Adirondacks

The number of single substances which have held the attention of every man in every age, recorded or remembered, is not large. Most of them have been the simplest and most basic necessities of life; flour to eat, clay for bricks with which to build houses, wool for warm clothing, copper and iron for implements, and timber for a thousand constructional purposes. Gold does not come into the category of simple and basic necessities.

None the less it has always been prominent in human thought. Few other things have succeeded as well as gold in tingeing metaphor, providing material for proverb, and creating legend.

Gold, Its Beauty, Power, and Allure
—C. H. Sutherland

—9—

Sluice Works

The miner's sluice box is a trough for washing gold-bearing gravel. As water is "sluiced" through, heavier gold grains are caught in the box's bottom. This bottom surface is fitted with riffles, and often under the riffles there will be some kind of particle-catching fabric, sometimes referred to as miner's moss.

We have been on a prospecting trip, have we not? It should not come as a surprise, then, that I here offer you a project in sluicing. Dr. Kelly has his gold file. I have one, too. I am now going to dump the contents of mine into the sluice box of this chapter. First is an amalgam of auriferous excerpts and brief summaries. Then there is a sampling of full-length newspaper articles reproduced from microfilm originals. Finally, I offer you a glimpse of the "life-cycle" of actual, once-incorporated North Country gold mines.

REFERENCES TO ADIRONDACK GOLD

Jackson Summit

A Professor Pfeifer of Durhamville, New York is described in this 1896 *Gloversville Daily Leader* article as a geologist of "wide and varied experience." Pfeifer, according to the *Leader*:

> ... has secured many specimens of free milling ores from the foothills in our immediate vicinity that show in gold from $10 to $20 per ton, and from the mine now being worked at Jackson Summit, specimens were obtained showing $200 per ton.... He [Pfeifer] also shows samples of ore from the old Mohawk Mine in St. Lawrence County that assay $460 in gold.[1]

Gold and Silver in the Town of Indian Lake

According to *History of Hamilton County:*

A claim for a mine containing gold and silver was filed by the Indian, Elijah Camp, with the Secretary of State in August 1889. An official assay, requested in November, proved highly encouraging. The location was given as 'three miles north of Indian Lake Village and one-half mile up the River from what is called Stanton's Point in Sherman's Township 17.'[2]

Gold in the Town of Parishville, St. Lawrence County

In my search for literary references to North County gold, I spent several days in the Oneida County Law Library, prospecting for any gold mine activity which involved litigation.

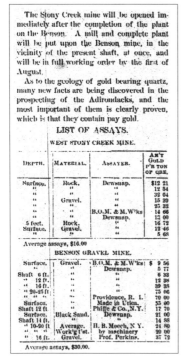

The Stony Creek mine will be opened immediately after the completion of the plant on the Benson. A mill and complete plant will be put upon the Benson mine, in the vicinity of the present shaft, at once, and will be in full working order by the first of August.

As to the geology of gold bearing quartz, many new facts are being discovered in the prospecting of the Adirondacks, and the most important of them is clearly proven, which is that they contain pay gold.

LIST OF ASSAYS.

WEST STONY CREEK MINE.

DEPTH.	MATERIAL.	ASSAYER.	AM'T GOLD P'R TON OF ORE.
Surface.	Rock.	Dewsnap.	$12 21
"	"	"	12 54
"	"	"	32 04
"	Gravel.	"	15 39
"	"	"	25 32
"	"	B.O.M. & M.W'ks	14 66
"	"	Dewsnap.	13 00
5 feet.	Rock.	"	16 72
Surface.	Gravel.	"	12 46
"	"	"	5 68

Average assays, $16.00

BENSON GRAVEL MINE.

Surface.	Gravel.	B.O.M. & M.W'ks	$ 9 56
"	"	Dewsnap.	5 77
Shaft 6 ft.	"	"	6 33
" 12 ft.	"	"	12 38
" 16 ft.	"	"	39 38
" 20-25 ft	"	"	75 06
Surface.	"	Providence, R. I.	70 00
" " "	"	Made in Utica.	55 00
Shaft 12 ft.	"	Phiffe & Co.,N.Y.	17 70
Surface.	Black Sand.	Dewsnap.	21 00
Shaft 14 ft.	"	"	14 88
" 10-20 ft	Average.	H. B. Meech, N Y.	24 80
" " "	Work'g l'st.	by machinery	20 00
" 16 ft.	Gravel.	Prof. Perkins.	37 72

Average assays, $30.00.

In the 1860s Goldmine Creek at mile 12.70 of the Northville Lake Placid Trail was a site of gold prospecting and mining, as the extraordinary rich assay would "seem" to indicate.

In the following excerpt from the legal publication, *Opinions Of The Attorney General*, notice how matter-of-factly Attorney General John J. Bennet, Jr., in his 1934 Opinion, establishes the existence of gold and silver on Macomb's Purchase:

> I am writing in answer to your [Conservation Department] letter of February 19 last, in which reference is made to a request to your department for permission to mine gold on the Forest Preserve.
>
> The site of the proposed gold mining project is on State-owned land in Lot 5. Twp.11, Great Tract 2, Macomb's Purchase, Town of Parishville, St. Lawrence County.
>
> …The State has always retained title to its gold and silver mines. 1 R.L., 1801, section 13, Kent and Radcliff; 1 R.L. 1813, 293, section 5, VanNess and Woodworth; 1 R.S. 1829, 198, section 5; Public Land Law, section 5, as amended.
>
> The Macomb Patent contains a reservation of gold and silver. Title to the mine in question is in the State and the land is a part of the State Forest Preserve. As such it is within the limitations set forth in article VII, section 7, of the State constitution so far as effective. It provides in part as follows: 'The land of the state, now owned or hereafter acquired, constituting the Forest Preserve as now fixed by law, shall be forever kept as wild forest lands. They shall not be leased, sold, or exchanged, nor shall the timber thereon be sold removed, or destroyed.'

Attorney General Bennet ultimately rules that the Conservation Department has no authority to issue a permit for the mining of gold on Forest Preserve land:

> Article VII, section 7, of the state constitution abrogates and nullifies the provision of the Public Lands Law, section 80, et seq., so far as Forest Preserve lands are concerned. The fact that no trees will be cut does not alter the situation.[3]

History of Lewis County

Under the "New Breman" heading this:

> On June 11, 1911, the Breman Reduction Company began building a 'gold plant' on property purchased from Mr. Ferdinand Andre who owned a farm on the Soft Maple Road near Bush Corners.

The plant was said to have utilized a 150-horsepower engine to turn flintstone-lined grinders which extracted gold residual from sand kernels. The Bremen Reduction Company operated from 1911 until 1915.

Two other gold plants were erected between Belfort and Long Pond in Croghan and operated in the summers of 1908, 1909, and 1910.[4]

"The Adirondack Gold Mines"

Preceding a list of assays taken from mines in the Benson Valley area, this 1882 *Gloversville Intelligencer* article begins:

> In the accompanying table of assays from the Adirondack mines, the particulars given are sufficiently full to demonstrate that pay gold exists in the vicinity from which they were taken.... What recommends these mines to all who investigate them is the general prevalence of gold in all their parts. It is not a strata here and there which bears gold, but there is good paying gold throughout the whole, from the very surface and increasing with depth. A handful of quartz gravel from the roadside, the plowed furrow, or the rivulet's bottom, over any part of hundreds of acres in this vicinity is sure to give gold, and in three cases out of five will show colors in the horn.

A table of assay results, including depth, assayer, and amount of gold per ton of ore is presented for four mines: the West Stony Creek Mill, the Benson Gravel Mine, the Otter Gulch Mine, and the Henry and Allen Mine. In all, thirty assay results by eight assay companies are reported with values ranging from $5.68 per ton to $75.06 per ton. The Benson Gravel Mine, according to the table results, is by far the richest mine.[5]

"Adirondack Eldorado"

In the literature about North Country gold, this is a must-read. Elizabeth Folwell, in a 1993 *Adirondack Life* story, provides a very informative, humorous overview of gold hunting in the Adirondacks. The prospecting activity that she writes about occurred between 1793 and the 1930s.

The author mentions numerous alleged gold discoveries. Among them are an 1879 placer find in Newton's Corners (now Speculator) by Ansel Scidmore; an 1890s discovery at Mount Pisgah by Saranac Lake blacksmith Edward Dobbins which assayed at $1.50 a ton; a 1930s find by an Algonquin Indian at Saranac Lake, which assayed at $15 a ton; a strike at Black Mountain. In each case the distinction between what is lode and what is lore is a little fuzzy. There is just enough of the historical here, though, to whet the appetite of anyone who finds sleuthing as exciting as sluicing.

Folwell mentions several notorious North Country gold mine scams as well. She concludes her essay with a pungent exhortation from a vintage *Engineering and Mining Journal* about gold-bearing sands:

> Not all of the Adirondack gold miners are swindlers: some of them are merely stupid.... Our advice is that Adirondack sand contains only green gold and that green gold is the stuff that gold bricks are made of.[6]

"About a Gold Mine in Ava"

This 1904 *Rome Daily Sentinel* story describes a gold discovery in Ava on the lands of Charles Willis and Lafayette Chase:

> Messrs. Willis and Chase have been experimenting in the production of gold from their lands, and last Saturday Mr. Willis was in Rome with a specimen of the gold which he secured. The specimen was about the size of the head of an ordinary pin and was exhibited in a cupel of bone. Mr. Willis says the gold is contained in a streak of gravel that crops out on the side of a deep gulf. To obtain the specimen he placed five pounds of gravel in a crucible and melted it in a brick arch.[7]

"Lure Of The Adirondack Gold"

Warwick Carpenter is the author of this twelve-page, 1911 narrative published in *The Outing Magazine*. His opening sentence: "News of the Black Mountain gold strike seized the entire northern slope of the Adirondacks in its pulsating grip and shook it out of a long winter's lethargy." Carpenter tells of a prospecting trip to the ridges overlooking Bog River. In the end what were thought to be pinhead-size nuggets of quartz gold turn out to be golden "eggs" laid by an inch worm! Mingled with the humor are some great descriptions of the Little Tupper/Bog River area. As well, there are some interesting, accurate prospecting tips about what real lode looks like.[8]

"Some Adirondack Gold Tales of the 'Brick' Variety"

George Alan Sturla, writing for the *Pine Log* in 1925, describes the driving nature of gold fever, even in the face of bleak pronouncements by geology experts and repeated failures of prospectors. Sturla begins:

> Ever since the dawn of civilization, man has been lured from the comfort and safety of his hearth and fireside to fields of hardship and danger encountered in the pursuit of that precious metal known as gold. For possession of this gleaming element he will murder and thieve. Hardships he will inflict upon others, even when the prospects of his attainment appear remotest; even when the tales of an El Dorado are of the most chimerical.

The author also features a sketch of Edward Dobbins, who having found evidence of gold on Pisgah Mountain, spent two consuming years trying to find the mother lode. He exhausted all of his finances and finally abandoned his efforts, never once losing belief that there was money to be made, if only he could drill deep enough.

Little credence is given to two other tales of gold mines in the vicinity of Saranac Lake Village.[9]

Gold Mine in the Village of Wells

Quoting Lewis L. Brownell of Northville, the Amsterdam *Evening Journal*, on August 5, 1880, offers the following:

> ... it is a well-known fact that parties operating in the vicinity of Wells, Hamilton County, sixteen miles from here, have found gold-bearing rock and are now engaged in sinking a shaft. The rock is shown by assay to contain both gold and silver. I am told that the vein showed, near the surface, five dollars in gold and three dollars in silver to the ton. As the sinking of the shaft progressed through dark quartz, the ore steadily increased in value and, at a depth of 35 feet, the assays showed $22 in gold and $2.50 in silver. The parties who are operating are experienced miners, and are very reticent as to quality, prospects, etc.... but claim to be perfectly satisfied with results so far.[10]

"Bleecker Rock Seems Likely to Pan Out Richly"

An 1898 *Gloversville Daily Leader* story reports that a gold-bearing ledge of rock located on the Gardner farm in Bleecker was blasted in order to obtain assay samples. A resulting test produced values from $12.50 to $15 a ton.[11]

"Finding Gold in New York State"

This 1898 *Scientific American* article by Cuyler Reynolds reports that:

> ... the Empire State has a well developed gold furor in the chase for the precious metal within its borders, and thousands of prospectors are excited by the finds in northern New York, and Hadley, Warren county seems to be the center of the territory now creating interest.

It is also stated that the gold-bearing sand which is milled at Hadley has a gold yield of $4 for each ton passed through the crusher and treated by a special cyanide chlorination process.[12]

Gold in Westernville, Boonville, and Ava

This 1905 *Rome Sentinel* article attempts to explain the assay process and how difficult it is to apply that process to the gold found in Western, Ava and Boonville because:

> … in this northern country several elements are present which hinder and prevent mining by any known process… such hinderances render all assays very unreliable, and prove if the ore can not be successfully assayed that all attempts to mine it on a large scale would be extreme folly.[13]

Gold and the Benson Gravel Mining Company

The introduction to this 1883 *Gloversville Intelligencer* article is most intriguing:

> Attention was first called to the existence of gold in the Adirondacks by a mysterious system of mining operations by a family named Belding. At regular periods during the last fifteen years the Beldings

have made trips to the mountains, taking with them gangs of men and tools for working in quartz. The ore thus gathered has been shipped to New York and there is reason to believe, notwithstanding the reticence of the Beldings, they have profited largely.

Included in this piece is a report from the Superintendent of the Benson Gravel Mining Company which cites the company's ability to remove gold-bearing gravel from their mine at the rate of 650 pounds every eight minutes. The article concludes:

> Too much cannot be said in praise of the Hoyt Bros. and their machine as produced by the Metropolitan Mining, Milling, and Manufacturing Co. The low price of their mill and the low cost at which it works the ore, and the large proportion of the gold saved, even in this region, where the bulk of the metal is 'flour' and 'float' places their mill far ahead of any preceding effort in gold mining and appears to be the inauguration of a new era in the mining of precious metals.[14]

The Rockhound's Manual and New York

In this 1972 "handbook for the gem an mineral collector," author Gordon S. Fay, under the heading, "Gold Discoveries in the United States," writes: "Gold has been found in many areas of the United States, but the term 'found' does not necessarily mean that the gold was always found in quantity." The author then presents a list titled, "Where Gold Has Been Found in the United States."

New York is in the list, and Fulton, Hamilton, and Saratoga Counties are cited as areas where "the rockhound has from a good to excellent chance of finding at least a little gold."[15]

"A Gold Plant in Operation Near Harrisville"

A Carthage correspondent writing for the *Rome Daily Sentinel* in 1904 reports on an operating gold extracting plant known as the Clear Creek Gold Mining Company. Walter Crocker, president of the company is quoted:

> Countless ages ago, during the ice period, the great glaciers of the north were slowly moving to the south. In their resistless march they

carried with them immense rocks which were dragged along and ground to pieces by the harder granite which they passed over in this country. It is for that reason that the tops of all the hills have that smooth appearance which they present.

The constant working back and forth ground the quartz into these minute particles and from them we obtain gold. There are many hundred thousand acres of this quartz in this section, all containing more or less gold.

Crocker then explains how amalgamators and quicksilver (mercury) are used in "the Corning Process" to extract the gold. One sample, according to Crocker, sent to Monroe, Hall and Hopkins, chemists and assayers of Washington, D.C., yielded 50 cents worth of gold for each pound of quicksilver. The reporter concludes:

> The mill, as constructed at present, will amalgamate 700 tons of sand per day with a very small force of men. There are millions of tons of sand in sight, and the company has rights enough to keep them running 25 years.[16]

Gold Mines in Fulton and Hamilton Counties

This 1882 Albany *Evening Journal* article reports on three areas where gold has been found: Benson Center, sixteen miles north of Gloversville and nine miles west of Northville; the vicinity of Wells and Lake Pleasant; an area northwest of Gloversville in Caroga.

Black sand from the site of the Benson Gravel Mining Company was assayed and found to contain gold at $7.63 a ton. It is further reported that multiple samples were taken from surface locations all along the Benson and tributary valleys and that assays ranged from $2 to $16 a ton.

Among incorporated gold mines in the area, according to this source are: the Benson Gravel Mining Company, the West Stony Creek Mining Company, the Adirondack Mining Company and the Albany Mining Company.[17]

Gold Mine on Dug Mountain

Under "Mining," the authors of *History of Hamilton County* state, without attaching a date, that "a mine shaft was early sunk on Dug Mountain. It penetrated the earth 85 feet and from it the owners drew both gold and silver."[18]

Mysterious Gold Mine at Piseco

According to *History of Hamilton County*:

> Over at Piseco, the Belden brothers came in search of gold and sank
> a mine of fifty feet on the south side of Belden Mountain near Spruce
> Lake. Above the shaft a dome was blown out overhead. The mine was
> worked by the Beldens with utmost secrecy over the years. Caroline
> Courtney, wife of Nathaniel Morril, used to tell how, when she was a little
> girl—she was born November 16, 1824—the Beldens took out the mineral
> by night in sealed barrels and boxes and transported it to the nearest rail-
> road station at Amsterdam.[19]

"Wealth In Rugged Rocks"

This 1906 *Rome Daily Sentinel* article profiles Peter F. Hugunine of
North Western. After years of research Hugunine is reported to have per-
fected a chemical process which is able to extract gold from a rock called
"fahlite, a combination of promiscuous metals not in their regular order."
Hugunine claims his method is able to produce a $100 per ton yield.
The article concludes with this upbeat prospecting forecast:

> The discoverer of this new process is naturally very much pleased
> with the success that has crowned his efforts after so long a period of
> research and experiment and believes that within the rugged rocks of
> northern Oneida County lies many a fortune ready to be worked out.[20]

Gold Near the Kunjamuck Trail

In *Adirondack Folks*, Ted Aber relates how Sabael Benedict would
cross to the east side of Indian Lake and head toward the Kunjamuck Trail
to Lake Pleasant. After some time he would return with a quantity of lead
which he used to make bullets. In 1826, incidentally, Sabael led David
Henderson, Duncan and Malcolm McMartin, John McIntyre, and Dyer
Thompson to the iron deposits of Tahawus.

Aber then states that Andrew Lackey of Warren County discovered
Sabael's secret source of lead in September of 1898. The mineral vein was
supposed to have been about a mile long and was located on "the southeast corner of a 2,000-acre lot in the northwest corner of Township #31 of

the Totten and Crossfield Purchase… between Lake Pleasant and Johnsburgh, about eleven miles from the Johnsburgh line."

Lackey apparently brought out a few pounds of his ore, had it tested, and found that along with a very pure grade of lead there was enough gold so that it could be extracted in paying quantities.[21]

Logger Stakes Claim

With a Massena dateline, this 1992 *Watertown Times* story reports that professional forester Thomas Taylor, owner of Star Lake Resources, was cruising a wood lot in the town of Fine when he discovered a "bright yellow streak cutting through the quartz rock."

Taylor sent assay samples to Nevada and California; the tests came back, showing gold and traces of silver. Taylor is quoted: "The vein is quite long. I followed it for several hundred feet and it breaks the surface all along. The lode may well go a mile." The *Times* further reports that a geologist told Taylor, "The Star Lake area is prime for gold and silver."

I saw Taylor's Notice of Discovery. It is one of the forty claims listed with the Secretary of State in "Folder 29" at Albany. Accompanying the claim, a photocopied Certificate of Assay from the R.L. Winkler Laboratory in Nevada shows values for gold at .018 ozs/ton, or about $5.40 per ton.[22]

A SAMPLING OF GOLD-RELATED ARTICLES
REPRODUCED FROM MICROFILM ORIGINALS

My literary prospecting involved many hours of searching through hundreds of reels of microfilmed, vintage newspapers. Just as a gold panner rejoices at the discovery of colors, so I found myself, after squinting at an endless, dizzying flow of microfilm, exulting every time I hit colors. One thing became apparent. Colors are there. You crank the viewer long enough, you find them. It's as simple as that.

EITHER GOLD OR HUMBUG.

THE ASSERTED DISCOVERY OF PAYING MINES IN NORTHERN NEW-YORK.

TROY, N. Y., July 26.—Claims for discoveries of gold mines in the Adirondack region are filed almost daily in the Secretary of State's office, in Albany. It may be that many interested persons are victims of a delusion, but it is certain that they believe that a new Eldorado exists in Northern New York. The hotels are overrun with gentlemen supposed to be capitalists who are quietly watching the developments , and have little to say. The Fonda, , Jamestown and Gloversville Railroad Company has employed an expert, who is making thorough search for valuable minerals, and he expresses the belief that there are many paying veins or leads in Fulton and Hamilton Counties, and several that have been discovered are said to promise very rich yields. ' Within the past year the interest has been constantly growing until at present it is nearly at fever heat, and gold is the one great topic of conversation in these counties. Wild rumors, as a natural consequence, are circulated, and claims and counter-claims are being made from day to day. Some persons are so greedy as to lay claim to a whole township, and one or tow have tried to capture a whole county in order to get the entire benefit of whatever bonanza is found to exist. Several instances have been noted where persons have resorted to "salting" ore and claiming a "find," thereby hoping to sell out at a fancy price.

At Wellstown there is a mine being worked by a company of Wisconsin men, which, from what can be learned, is paying well. The company is working at it steadily, and those interested are very reticent as to what success they are meeting with. But that they are satisfied with past results and confident of a great future is evidenced by the fact that they have refused all offers from persons wishing to buy stock, and are keeping it all to themselves, and further, that they have recently increased the wages of their employees, and have ordered extensive machinery, with which to complete the work of reducing and refining on their own grounds. It is reported on good authority that the company is realizing $150 a ton from the ore. A rich vein has also been discovered under the jail at Lake Pleasant, within the corporation limits of the village of Northville, in Fulton County. This the expert alluded to pronounces the richest vein found. Pieces picked up at random on the surface have been assayed by J. D. Marsh, Government Assayer, and found to average $13.34 gold, and $1.75 silver, a total valuation of $15.09 to the ton. It is the opinion of the expert that the deeper this vein is penetrated the richer it will grow, and that it will prove the best paying vein in the region, although only a few yards distant, by the side of a brook, in blasting for a spring, another vein has been discovered, specimens from which have been assayed by two assayers, each of whom found his specimen to show a valuation of more than $1,000 to the ton. The ore is much darker than that from which gold is taken in western mines, but some of it is no doubt very rich in gold, with a paying quantity of silver and a liberal sprinkling of lead and other minerals. Either gold mines which it will pay to work have been discovered, or one of the most skillful confidence operations of the age has been developed.

The New York Times, July 27, 1880

58

THE GOLD FIELDS OF NEW-YORK.

SOME OF THE CHARACTERISTIC BEAUTIES OF THE NORTHVILLE CAMP GROUNDS.

CAMP GROUNDS, NORTHVILLE, Aug. 14.— Here in Northern New-York, situated on the west side of the Sacondaga River, and just opposite the picturesque little village of Northville, are the camp grounds of the Saratoga District of the Troy Conference. Though occupied for a number of years, it seems that during the past three seasons their popularity has received an unusual impetus. They are now attracting attention from many parts of the State, and their annual gatherings have quite superseded in importance those of the Round Lake Association. It is understood that the latter is heavily indebted, which fact, together with the sale of its grounds under a decree of foreclosure, have so badly crippled it that no meeting will be held under its management during the present season. Northville is nestled among the hills of the Adirondack region, is about half a mile from the grounds, and has a population of 1,200. With its main street, a mile long, containing rows of flourishing forest maples, its high altitude and bracing atmosphere, it is one of the most healthful Summer retreats in the State. Though settled at an early day, it is still on the very confines of the Northern wilderness, a few hours' journey bringing the traveler right into the midst of a dense and interminable forest, extending to the waters of the St. Lawrence, and being the largest belt of timber land in the United States outside of Washington Territory. It is about 30 miles from the New-York Central, with which it is connected by the Fonda, Johnstown, and Gloversville, and the Fonda, Johnstown, Gloversville and Northville Railroads. The latter road is an extension of the former, and the two are known as one thoroughfare.

The camp grounds contain over a hundred handsome cottages, and perhaps an equal number of tents. The railway runs through the grove, leaving passengers within a stone's throw of the auditorium. A commodious hotel, an excellent restaurant, and most of the modern conveniences, excepting, perhaps, a bar, are at hand. A gentleman from Boston has recently invested a number of thousands of dollars in a large tract of land skirting the river bank. He is now making an outlay of $10,000 more on its improvement. This will consist of walks, drives, fountains, and a beautiful park. The balance of the land he has cut into small lots, which he is rapidly selling at $100 each. A number have already erected cottages on these, which are built at an expense of about $150 each. They are sold to persons who desire a nice, quiet Summer resort, where economy and not fashion is the ruling consideration. Among the occupants of cottages is the Rev. Washington Frothingham known as "The Hermit of New-York." These cottages, together with the numerous tents, have been occupied by private families during the greater part of the Summer, including a number of New-Yorkers. An estimate made last week placed such occupants at 1,000 persons, exclusive of visitors.

This vicinity is also the seat of the gold district of Northern New-York. Five hundred claims have been filed with the Secretary of State, including one for the bottom of Lake Pleasant, and another for the whole of Gloversville, a flourishing inland village of 7,000 inhabitants. Some miles south of here innumerable companies have been formed, shafts sunk, machinery and appliances procured, and every other man seems to enjoy the privilege of showing his specimen ore. From an old gentleman once distinguished as a Justice of the Peace, I gained the following bit of legendary information: Many years ago an individual, supposed to be of Spanish blood, delved among the hills and rocks of this locality for several years, at the end of which time he suddenly disappeared, leaving nothing behind but a rumor that he had removed a large quantity of the precious metal. This supposition was confirmed by the recognition that a magic spell for a long time afterward pervaded the locality, evidently the work of some Genii for the purpose of preventing the curious from learning more of the stranger's researches. About this time my informant (to use his own language) started to investigate the matter. As he was riding thoughtfully over a piece of boggy land, there suddenly appeared in close proximity to his horse's head an Indian chieftain, a grand-looking fellow, dressed in full head gear and other native paraphernalia. The Squire's horse stopped, and he was about to address the apparation, when lo! it disappeared, leaving him so startled that he lost all memory of the locality, and repeated search never enabled him to find it. He is now an old man, but this adventure of his early days has left a lasting impression on his mind. He is very much exercised over "the new version," and very impatient at the delay of the revisors of the Old Testament Unless a more definite Biblical account can be given of the land of Ophir, he is certain that that interesting spot must be in this locality.

The river is dotted with tiny boats, which are much used by the visitors; good fishing and hunting is found, an excellent police system has been inaugurated, and any desiring may have the right of squatter's sovereignty for a spot large enough for tent or cottage. The railroad company is very accommodating, and its officers are men of the highest character. The meetings opened on Monday evening, and incoming trains during the week so far have unloaded thousands of persons on the grounds. It is evident, however, that most of the cottage occupants, as well as the visitors, are more interested in enjoying the delightful atmosphere and beautiful mountain scenery than in their spiritual welfare; at least the Presiding Elder, the Rev. Thomas Griffin, of Saratoga, i; under this impression, and has frequently so expressed himself during the meetings. But few old-fashioned Methodists are here, and these are very apprehensive that the grounds may degenerate into a large pleasure garden for city people during the Summer months. Consumption and asthma are foreign terms here; pretty girls in swinging hammocks are numerous, and groups of both Jews and Gentiles are seen standing near the trunks of grand old trees, utterly unmindful that religious services are being held. Everything bids fair to make this little mountain retreat permanently popular.

New York Times, August 16, 1883

GOLD IN TWO COUNTIES.

Auriferous Deposits in Both Oneida and St. Lawrence.

Peter F. Hugunine, who resides some ten miles south of Boonville village, has discovered a vein of gold on lands not so very far from his own property. He says that the land is not for sale and consequently he doubtless has an option on it. Mr. Hugunine, who is something of a mineralogist, has been at work on details connected with the discovery for no little time. He has had the quartz assayed and finds that it yields about $60 to the ton and that it also contains a quantity of silver, both rich in quality. The indications point to a rich mine and when the snow melts a few feet the parties interested are to work the mine for all it is worth.

Gold has also been discovered on the rocky farm of J. Lincoln Hockens of DePeyster, St. Lawrence county. The matter has been kept a secret until recently awaiting the report of an expert assayer. This report places the ore at a value of $75 a ton. Mr. Hockens has already commenced mining on a small scale and has taken out a ton and a half of gold bearing quartz. The vein was found near the surface of the ground and runs into the side of a hill. Expert miners say the find is a valuable one. Preparations are being made for extensive mining operations in the spring.

Boonville Herald and Adirondack Tourist
February 13, 1902

GOLD AND SILVER FOUND

ALONG LANSING KILL AND MOHAWK RIVER.

P. F. Hugunine Perseveres in His Prospecting—Deposits Located Between Lock 70 and Wells' Creek on the Black River Canal in Lime and Slate Rocks.

P. F. Hugunine, who is interested in locating and mining gold and silver ore between Wells' Creek and lock 70 on the Black River canal, along the Lansing Kill and the Mohawk river, says that he has made thorough tests there and finds both minerals. The ore deposits are in rocks, which lie in blanket form, in that locality. Lafayette Chase, on whose premises the test mill is located, and Charles Willis, are interested in the work. The test mill consists of furnaces, crusher and concentrator.

The gold and silver are deposited in rocks that are commonly known as lime and slate stone. The mill consists of a crusher that crushes the rocks, which are then smelted with a crucible furnace. This reduces several metals with the gold and silver, which appear more or less alloyed in small heads that are suspended in the melted mass called a slag. The slag is then crushed and placed in a concentrating machine which separates the metals from the slag. The metals are then cupeled in a muffle furnace the usual way, which process leaves gold, silver and platinum only. The machines are driven by water power. Mr. Hugunine has samples of both silver and gold taken from about ten pound runs.

In the samples which he has with him are contained nearly a pennyweight of gold. The pure gold is of a beautiful characteristic yellow. It has the amber colors peculiar to the Black river country.

The frequent rains have greatly hindered in the work of prospecting and the first run was made last week.

Mr. Hugunine has as yet opened no mine but simply prospected and experimented with the rock which has eroded from the outcrop. He expects eventually to open a mine.

Boonville Herald and Adirondack Tourist
July 24, 1902

ECHOES OF ADIRONDACKS

VALUABLE SAMPLES THAT COME
FROM BIG MOOSE LAKE.

Sections of the Adirondacks Said to
Be Rich With the Precious Metal—
Prospects of a Klondike Near Our
Door.

It begins to look as though there would be a rush for gold nearer Albany than the Klondike pretty soon. Men, prominent in mining enterprises, are looking toward the Adirondacks for the future field of action. It is said that sands that have been treated there will yield as much as $60 a ton, which is unusually high. "Paydirt" as low as $8 and even $4 a ton is considered profitable.

For the last few months men representing a group of Philadelphia capitalists have been collecting samples of sand from along the lakes and streams in the country between Lake Champlain and Lake Ontario for the purposes of having them treated by an improved chlorination process. The results have been so satisfactory that the Philadelphians want to lease, buy or get options on a lot of sand. Sands showing values from $8 to $60 a ton are from samples that come from the shores of Big Moose Lake in Herkimer county. If there is much of this $60 a ton stuff the Big Moose Lake country is a second Eldorado. There are comparatively few mines in the world that give values of $60 to the ton of ore. So impressed are the Philadelphia people with what has been shown thus far that they are building a dredge to scour the lake, their theory being that they will get richer sand in the bed of the lake than along the shore. That there is gold in the Adirondack country was known a century ago. Locks, in his treatise on gold (pages 180-181), says that there are four well defined fields. The treatise, which was published in London more than a quarter of a century ago, says the gold belt begins about Plattsburg and runs south into Hamilton, Fulton and Saratoga counties and branches west through Herkimer and east into Washington county. Gold is found in at least ten counties in the northern part of the state, the whole region between the Canadian border and Lake Ontario being within the gold district. Half a dozen times within the last twenty or thirty years samples of sand taken from the various spots in the Adirondack country have known, when tested in the laboratories, a perentage of gold valued all the way from $4 to $8 a ton.

The Philadelphia people sent to Albany to look up mining claims filed in this state and were astonished to discover that there were 10,000, most of

Boonville Herald and Adirondack Tourist, May 14, 1908. Continued on page 61

them being in the Adirondack belt. A lot of these claims have lapsed—probably 95 per cent or more.

Recent history of gold mining in New York state dates back nearly 30 years. Then it was that William T. Bullis of Glens Falls announced that he had discovered gold in paying quantities in sands near that town. Finding that the fire assay test, to which gold-bearing material always is put, did not give satisfactory results in the case of the sand, he invented a barrel amalgamator of his own and used cobblestones and water in his amalgamating process. He kept up his experiments till his death. Soon afterwards Dr. C. P. Bellows, a Gloversville dentist, had a sample of black sand, which he had obtained from a neighboring stream, assayed, and it is said that it showed $7.63 in gold per ton. He also did a great deal of experimenting, even building a small test mill near Gloversville but he was never successful. Other prospectors were Charles O. Yale of Yale lock fame, and Alonzo Chase of Redfield, S.D. The latter asserted that he obtained an average of $4 in gold per ton from several hundred samples of sand from Hamilton and Fulton counties.

In the year 1896 a sample of sand from Essex County was reported as bearing $27 worth of gold and $1.11 worth of silver per ton, and another sample from Saratoga county was declared to show $34 in gold per ton. These reports created quite a bit of excitement and many persons hastened to file claims for property in Northern New York. In the two years following, claims to the number of 3-000 were filed with the secretary of state from Saratoga, Essex, Fulton, Herkimer, Warren, and Lewis counties.

Boonville Herald and Adirondack Tourist, May 14, 1908. Continued from page 60

GOLD STRIKE IN ADIRONDACKS.

Reported Discovery of Rich Deposit In Essex County, Near Lake Placid.

Lake Placid, May 12.—Accompanied by F. A. Isham, his attorney, Henry Allen of Lake Placid, deputy sheriff of Essex County, is in Albany in an effort to finally establish his claim to what is thought by competent experts to be a rich gold deposit.

A short time ago Mr. Allen returned to Lake Placid from a long trip through a little frequented section of the Adirondacks. With him he brought a number of samples of gold bearing ore which he exhibited to a few close friends. Thursday he returned from another such trip, and Friday he started for Albany, Mr. Isham departing later to join him there.

Before leaving Mr. Allen confided to friends in Lake Placid that one object of his trip is to file in the office of the secretary of state a claim to the gold mine he believes he has found. The vein has been opened for about 800 feet and appears to be of a rich and even quality. Samples of the ore taken from the ledge Mr. Allen has discovered were sent by him to New York, where they were tested by representatives of the Guggenheims, and are said to have assayed as high as $40,000 to $70,000 a ton, a value which experts declare has never before been reached by vein ore.

According to reports circulated Mr. Allen, his attorney, and his brother, Eugene Allen, will confer in Albany with representatives of the Guggenheims and New York banking house.

Mr. Allen's reported discovery is the climax of a considerable period of speculation and rumors regarding the finding of gold in the mountains. It was only a short time ago that John Clark, who has lived some distance from Lake Placid for many years, was reported to have found gold bearing ore. Eugene Allen, brother of the deputy sheriff, was then credited with the discovery. Sheriff Allen's own discovery is, however, quite apart from the undertakings of either his brother or Mr. Clark, and has created no end of excitement among people in Lake Placid and surrounding villages in the Adirondacks. Gold hunters from these places are preparing to search the woods for traces of the precious metal.

That there is gold in the mountains has long been the firm belief of many persons. Five years ago a party of men from the United States Geodetic Survey found unmistakable traces of it in small quantities near the head of Tupper Lake, and about the same time workmen in the employ of George A. Stevens and his brother, John Stevens, of Lake Placid, uncovered a small vein of ore in the southern part of Lake Placid, which assayed heavily when submitted to test by J. N. Stower, superintendent of the iron mines at Lyon Mountain.

Boonville Herald and Adirondack Tourist, May 13, 1909. Courtesy Ted Comstock

GOLD IN BLACK RIVER SAND

COMER REFINING COMPANY FILES PAPERS—CAPITALIZED AT $100,000.

Headquarters at Lowville—Firm Interested Primarily in Development of Lewis County Claims Through New Process.

Lowville, Sept. 12.—The certificate of incorporation of the Comer Refining Company of New York has been filed in the office of the Secretary of State and the office of the County Clerk of Lewis County. The Company, which has its principal office in Lowville, is capitalized at $100,000, divided into 1,000 shares of the par value of $100 each.

The shares are held as follows: Joseph A. Comer, Lowville, 500 shares; Charles R. Harris, Los Angeles, Cal., 1 share; B. J. Hatmaker, Lowville, 497 shares; R. B. Hough, Lowville, 1 share; Kate A. Comer, Lowville, 1 share. The shareholders above mentioned also constitute the Board of Directors of the company for the first year.

The purpose of the company, as stated in the certificate of incorporation, is to buy, sell and deal in gold, silver and other metals, bullion, precipitates, concentrates and other materials containing gold, silver and other metals; to mine, develop and extract gold, silver and other metals from sand, gravel and rocks of the State of New York, and to do general mining, milling, smelting and refining business; to own, buy, sell, acquire by condemnation under the public land law of the State of New York mines and mineral rights, deal in, develop and work such mineral rights and mining claims in the State of New York; to own, buy, sell and deal in real estate; to own, buy, sell and deal in the stock, bonds and other evidences of debt of other corporations, domestic or foreign, and to issue therefor its stock, bonds or other obligations as provided by Section 52 of the stock corporation law of the State of New York.

In this connection, it is stated that the company is interested primarily in the development of the so-called gold mining claims located east of the Black River in Lewis county. These claims are nearly all located in the towns of Croghan and New Bremen in the county of Lewis.

The company maintains that the sand of which these claims consist is rich in gold, and that the precious metal can be recovered in paying quantities by a process which the company is using. A laboratory for the making of tests has been fitted up in the Fowler Brothers' storehouse in Exchange street in this village.

Boonville Herald and Adirondack Tourist, September 15, 1910

63

GOLD IN THE ADIRONDACKS
CLAIMS FILED BY WILLIAM CRONK OF ROME

There have been many rumors afloat lately to the effect that gold had been discovered in the Adirondack region. Many people living in the vicinity of the big woods doubt the fact that gold is to be found there and regard the stories and rumors as illusions and cite the fact that different parties have been working in the vicinity of Croghan, Lewis County, but as yet have been unable to demonstrate the fact that gold can be extracted or separated from the sands found there on a paying basis, although one party of capitalists has expended nearly $10,000 in erecting a plant for that purpose.

A few days ago William Cronk of Rome, son of the late Hiram Cronk, last survivor of the War of 1812, who has been a guide in the Adirondacks for nearly 50 years made the statement that he has had positive knowledge that there was gold in the Adirondacks for many years, having had assays made in Albany by Mr. Hall, state geologist, over 30 years ago which showed over $30 to the ton. When asked why he had not made some effort to mine or work it he said, "he did not know how to go about it as well as he did to kill a bear," and he had put it off year after year waiting for some favorable opportunity. Now he has got along in years and pretty well stiffened up by rheumatism and has made arrangements whereby his two sons, Hiram and William O. Cronk, and Rae A. Edgerton will have full control and be in a position to work the various claims that have been filed by Mr. Cronk in Herkimer, Lewis and Oneida Counties.

When asked if he had discovered any gold in Oneida County Mr. Cronk answered in the affirmative. He said he had found gold in the sands nearly the whole length of Fish Creek and that he has claims filed covering a good share of its banks extending through Lewis and Oneida Counties. He has had several essays made on the sands in this vicinity which have shown values ranging from 50 cents to $10 per ton of sand. Mr. Cron has traveled on foot over nearly every acre of ground from Fish Creek to Lake Champlain between the Mohawk and St. Lawrence Rivers.

When asked his opinion as to there being gold in and around Croghan, he referred the inquiry to Rae Egerton who has spent nearly four weeks investigating the situations in that vicinity for the purpose of determining how a concentrating apparatus he has been perfecting would work the material found there. Mr. Edgerton claims to have made many tests on the sand found around Croghan, Belfort, Jerden Falls and vicinity and found the results entirely satisfactory.

But he states that there is an element in the sands there which is puzzling. Assays made on small portions of sand with chemicals make a very good showing, but when working on an extensive scale a different proposition presents itself. Values can be extracted from gold bearing sand ore either chemically or mechanically. What is known as the cyanide process has been tried in Croghan without success and several mercurial processes have been tried, but none were what had been hoped for on account of an element that causes the mercury to sicken (loses its power to pick up the gold). Consequently there is much loss in values.

Mr. Edgeton believes from his experience that the only economical method by which the values can be saved from he sand in that vicinity is a mechanical process. He claims to have perfected a concentrating apparatus which will save at least 95 per cent of any mineral entering it, the specific gravity of which is one per cent heavier then the gangue. He claims that by using this process for concentrating and then passing the concentrates through another process he can save practically all the values in an economical manner and run on a good paying basis.

It has been proven by many chemical tests that gold is there. It only remains to install the right process to separate it from the sands successfully.

Mr. Edgerton and E. Burdick from Belfort, who has a number of claims filed in the Adirondack region, and has been a prospector and followed mining for a number of years, made a number of tests on sands from Boonville, Forestport, Ava, Lee, and Lyons Falls last week. They found in every case traces of gold, more or less, and also that the samples showed from 50 to 500 pounds of magnetite to the ton, which is worth on the market in the neighborhood of $10 dollars per ton. They believe that there is enough magnetite to pay operating expenses outside of what gold can be saved.

Mr. Egerton and several others are expecting to begin operations on quite an extensive scale as soon as spring opens and are making plans to that end.

Boonville Herald and Adirondack Tourist, December 2, 1909. Courtesy Ted Comstock

GOLD DEPOSITS IN NORTHERN NEW YORK

Platinum and Copper Found in the Black River District

A dispatch from Syracuse, published in the New York Tribune says:

Deposits of platinum, copper and gold worth probably millions of dollars, lie in the limestone rock foundations in the Black River district in Northern New York, roughly bounded by Watertown, Lowville and Gouverneur, according to E. C. Jordan of this city, chemist, assayist and metallurgist.

"The deposits are in such quantities that they can be detected in many places with simple, crude field tests with drops of acid and with very small pieces of rock being used. In laboratory tests with small amounts of material under examination deposits have been found indicating a yield of one ounce of precious metals per ton, about one-half of which was platinum metal. At this rate it is estimated the rock from which the samples were secured would run from $70 per ton upward.

"The finding of this amount of precious metal in the samples brought to Syracuse has convinced Mr. Jordan that somewhere in the territory from which they came are large deposits of platinum. He will not hazard a guess as to their approximate size or their value. He merely says he is convinced there are large deposits.

Made Hundreds of Tests

"Mr. Jordan has made hundreds of tests during a period of seven years. He is a former resident of Gouverneur and has gone over the entire territory on foot several times. He has checked over the analysis of other chemists and has reached his conclusion only after the most exhaustive and intensive study of the situation.

"He is not financially interested in the matter in any way. He owns no property in or near Watertown, has no financial interests there and is not connected with any company, corporation or any other concern in or near that city interested in the matter in any way. He makes his statement simply as a matter of news as the result of repeated examinations and tests, and with a desire to inform the people of Northern New York of the gigantic possibilities he believes are lying underneath their homes.

"When a resident of Gouverneur he had many occasions to test samples of limestone for friends and business concerns in that section, mostly for magnesia and lime. He discovered that in many cases these results would be prevented from coming out accurately by the presence of other substances. He discovered it was necessary to remove these metals before he could conclude his original tests. This puzzled him. Finally he put it down as a peculiarity of the rock formation of that district, and let it go at that.

Found Platinum Metal

"However, after coming to Syracuse curiosity prompted him one day to make further investigations as to the cause of this peculiar reaction. He extracted the precious metal deposit and analyzed it, with the result that he found the copper and platinum metals.

"As to the quantity of the deposits of platinum he has found in his laboratory tests, he points out that in these examinations he uses only one gram of material.

"Another peculiarity of the Northern New York ores which he has discovered is that the usual methods of testing by fire and melting are absolutely worthless. This method is the one used extensively in treatment of nearly all western ores and works very successfully. With the Northern New York ores, however, all the precious metal deposits are in the slag and not shown. He has, therefore, been forced to use other processes. He makes no effort to explain this characteristic of the Northern New York formations."

Boonville Herald and Adirondack Tourist, July 28, 1921, 1910

THE RISE AND FALL OF ADIRONDACK GOLD MINES

In the late 1800s and the early 1900s a number of North Country gold mining companies were incorporated. A sampling follows:

Adirondack Mining Company
Albany Mining Company
Comer Refining Company
Benson Gravel Mining Company
Bremen Reduction Company
Indian River Gold Mining Company
Iridium-Platinum Gold Mining Company
Mount Tom Gold Mining Company
Mohawk Mining Company
Fahrig and Sons Mining
Riverside Gold Mining and Reduction Company
Sacandaga Mining and Milling Company
Twentieth Century Gold Extracting Company
West Stony Creek Mining Company

While a few of these mining operations were bogus from the start, many were good-faith (perhaps extreme-faith is the more appropriate descriptor) enterprises. They were companies that were organized in accord with New York State corporation law. Company owners believed, sometimes blindly and obsessively, that schemes of hugely profitable gold production were entirely reasonable and workable.

It seems to me that the life cycle of a North Country gold mine progressed through five stages:

In the first stage a contagion of gold fever sweeps through the populace at large. Epidemic excitement churned up by spectacular gold finds in California and Alaska spreads to New York. If there is gold in the rugged Klondike, why not in some of the oldest mountains on the planet? There is no reason to think that the Adirondacks are not hiding vast stores of precious metals. It is simply a matter of time before some persistent prospectors hit serious pay dirt.

The glittering specimen is produced in the second stage. It is verified as a bona fide, geologically local specimen, and is determined by reputable assayers to be worth, say, $50 of gold per ton of ore. The specimen emits a golden gleam that is picked up by the retinal photo-receptors of the gazing human eye. The optic nerve fires raw auriferous data straight to the brain. Eight nanoseconds later a burning question arises from the cerebral cortex: how can I get in on commercially mining this stuff and be a lucky beneficieary of the Adirondack El Dorado?

In the third stage, like-minded speculators, informed by the irrefutable gleam of genuine gold, carefully appraise the odds. They form companies, file certificates of incorporation, sell stocks, and spend thousands of dollars erecting buildings and buying equipment. Untold quantities of ore are milled and assayed. Responsible, savvy, knowledgeable men often assumed the corporate helm. The president of the Riverside Gold Mining and Reduction Company of St. Regis Falls, New York, was Congressman William Henry Flach. His fellow investors included a mining engineer, two physicians, a high school principal, a former State Assemblyman, and at least three well-known and successful businessmen.

Fourth, the mining company does not produce one authentic troy ounce of gold, ever. Undaunted, incessantly hopeful investors persevere, and persevere, and persevere. The total suspension of disbelief stubbornly prevails.

Finally, after having poured huge sums of money into deep shafts and gravel pits and stream beds and mountainsides and seas of Adirondack "gold-bearing" sand, the gold mine owners inexorably default on taxes for three consecutive years. The New York Department of State quietly snuffs out the corporation via an unhappy legal instrument stamped "DISSOLVED BY [TAX] PROCLAMATION," copies of which follow:

Wen the undersigned, all being of full age and two- thirds being citizens of the Uni
States and one of us a resident of the State of New York, for the purpose of forming a
corporation under the BUSINESS CORPORATION LAW of the State of New York, do hereby cert
and set forth:

FIRST:- The name of said Corporation shall be
"HARRISVILLE MINING COMPANY".

SECOND.? The purposes for which said corporation is to be formed are as follows:

(L) to buy, lease or otherwise acquire mines, mining rights, quarries and mineral l
every kind, nature and description, and to work, mine, prospect, develop, operate and
mobe the same; to mine, quarry and excavate copper, gold, silver, zinc and other ores

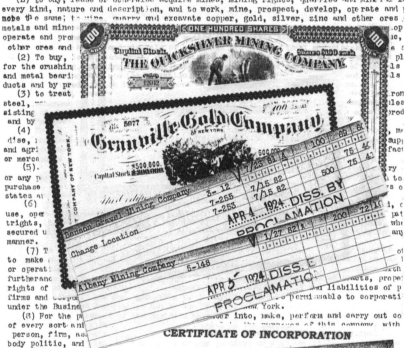

metals and mine   op
operate and pro   ie,
other ores and   e s
(2) To buy,   pl
for the crushing   ls
and metal beari   ls
ducts and by pr
(3) to treat   ron
steel,   les
sisting   rod
and by
(4)   m
dise,   sup
and agri   fac
or merca
(5).   ry
or any p   to
purchase   s o
states a
(6)
use, oper   1, c
trights,   pat
secured u   wh
manner.   any
(7) T   o
to make   1
or operati   ch
furtheranc   ts, prope
rights of   liabilities of p
firms and   permissable to corporati
under the Busine   w York.
(8) For the p   er into, make, perform and carry out co
of every sort an   purposes of this company, with
person, firm, as
body politic, and

CERTIFICATE OF INCORPORATION

thereof.
(9) To do any or al   We, the undersig   V
to purchase, acquire,   thirds being citizens o
ness of any corporatic   residents of the State
stocks or other oblig   Corporation pursuant
IN WITNESS WHEREOF,   State of New York, do
of August, one thousar   this certficate for that
FIRST. The name o   posed corporation is "COMER
State of New York, Cou   REFINING COMPANY OF NEW YORK."
On this 2nd   SECOND: The purposes for which this corporation is formed
A. Crimmins, William N   are to buy, sell and deal in gold, silver, and other metals, bullion,
mentioned and describe   precipitates, concentrates, and other material containing gold,
acknowledged to me the   silver and other metals, to mine, develop and extract gold, silver
$5.00   and other metals from sands, gravels and rocks of the State of
Received from Harr New York, and to do a general mining, milling,, smelting and
twentieth of one per   refining business; to own, buy, sell and deal in the stock and
company, for the priv

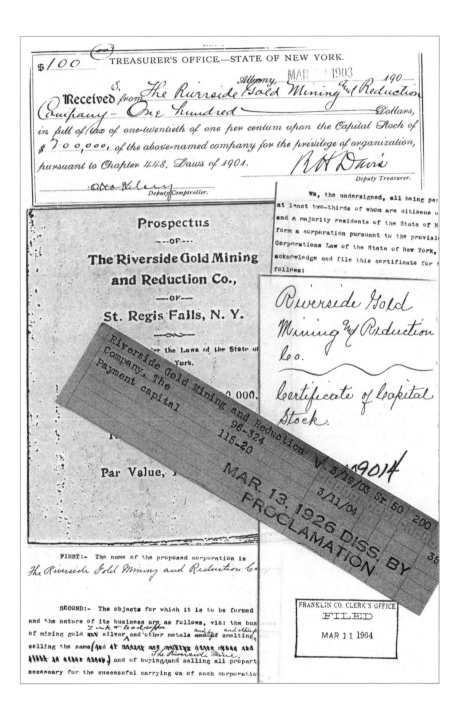

$100

TREASURER'S OFFICE.—STATE OF NEW YORK.

Albany, MAR 1903 190

Received from *The Riverside Gold Mining and Reduction Company* — *One hundred* Dollars,

in full of tax of one-twentieth of one per centum upon the Capital Stock of

$ 200,000, of the above-named company for the privilege of organization,

pursuant to Chapter 448, Laws of 1901.

R H Davis
Deputy Treasurer.

Deputy Comptroller.

We, the undersigned, all being per
at least two-thirds of whom are citizens o
and a majority residents of the State of N
form a corporation pursuant to the provisi
Corporations Law of the State of New York,
acknowledge and file this certificate for
follows:

Prospectus

---OF---

The Riverside Gold Mining

and Reduction Co.,

---OF---

St. Regis Falls, N. Y.

Riverside Gold
Mining and Reduction
Co.

Certificate of Capital
Stock.

... er the Laws of the State of
York.

0,000.

Par Value,

Riverside Gold Mining and Reduction
Company. The
Payment capital

96-324
115-20

MAR. 13. 1926 DISS. BY
PROCLAMATION

V. 3/19/03. Sr. 50 200

3/11/04

35

FIRST:— The name of the proposed corporation is
The Riverside Gold Mining and Reduction Co

SECOND:— The objects for which it is to be formed
and the nature of its business are as follows, viz: the bus
Zinc + lead-copper   and by   and other
of mining gold and silver, and other metals and for smelting,
The Riverside Mine
selling the name and to smelt any mining metal ores and
pure in other ores, and of buying and selling all propert
necessary for the successful carrying on of such corporation

FRANKLIN CO. CLERK'S OFFICE
FILED
MAR 11 1904

Why is gold so pale? Because it has so many thieves plotting against it.

Epigram
—Diogenes

—10—

The Bre-X Factor

The Biblical axiom is "The love of money is the root of all evil." Out of that axiom flows the Bre-X Factor: "Any sustained period of gold fever will always produce bunco artists and victims."

One day in a remote part of Indonesia some Australian prospectors happened to notice Dayak tribespeople panning for gold along a river in northeast Borneo. The rest is history, yet history so recent it is but a click away on the Internet. Two men, experienced field geologists, claimed to have found, in the middle of Borneo's Busang Jungle, the biggest mother lode on the planet, 200 million ounces of gold, worth about 70 billion dollars. The geologists worked for a small mining firm in Canada, Bre-X Minerals, Ltd.

Subsequent advertisements by Bre-X in the Fall of 1996 triggered a massive frenzy of gold fever. Thousands of investors dumped millions of dollars into the money-maker of a lifetime, the world's greatest gold find. Suddenly the giant green bubble burst.

Stockholders, suspicious that ore samples had been salted, arranged for additional samples to be assayed. The results were conclusive. There was no mother lode. Nor was there a daughter lode nor a third-cousin lode. The Bre-X gold find turned out to be a colossal fraud. By May 1997 stock that had sold for $200 a share was selling for seven cents. The mega-hoax would eventually bilk investors out of six billion dollars.

One of the two mine discoverers, Michael de Guzman, mysteriously stepped out of an airborne helicopter on his way to answer questions about Bre-X testing methods. His body was found four days later, face decomposed, internal organs eaten by wild boars.[1] The other architect of the scam, John Felderhof, is apparently proclaiming innocence… from the safety of his home in the Cayman Islands, where he will no doubt spend a bit of the thirty million dollars he scammed. The Bre-X Factor.

Scientists have known for a long time that the oceans contain gold,

LEWIS COUNTY GOLD MINES

Lyon Falls People Have Possibly Struck It Rich

Considerable exitement prevailed in Lyon Falls when it was announced that the sample sent by L. H. Stewart from his possible gold mine in New York for assay purposes was reported by the assayer to be that previous metal. The sample sent for testing weighed 1 pound and 2 ounces and the report gives the value of the same at $285.24 of gold per ton and $4.27 of silver. The value of the test is so high as to give rise to the suspicion that the find had been "salted," so says the assayer. It is reported that crowds of men from all over the county daily visit the new Klondike and are even busily staking out claims by the light of lanterns before dawn and after nightfall as well as through every hour of the day. All sorts of conditions of men flock to the gold mine, farmers, artisans, tradesmen and the clergy. In some cases claims have been staked not only by and for the heads of families but for every individual member of those families from infant Tommy to grown up Susie. War talk is at a discount and should the Spanish land in New York today our patriots would be found in "the diggins." So many samples of that which glitters have been sought on the Stewart claim, that that gentleman has found it necessary to watch his posessions armed with a shot gun. Copies of state mining laws and laws governing claims have been secured from the secretary of state and are the subject of close study. Those wishing to examine specimens need not give themselves the tedium of a pilgrimage to this mecca of hopes and fears, but may have their curiosity satisfied by making application to the office of the grist mill in this village, where samples may be viewed with the aid of a magnifying glass free of charge. Messrs. Anderson, Burrell & Snell, said to be mining experts from abroad visited the gold region Saturday. It is said that this valuable discovery was made through the agency of a dream and the instrumentality of a fortune telling Sibyl.

Boonville Herald and Tourist, April 28, 1898

MORE GOLD DISCOVERIES.

. Ever and anon there are reported discoveries of gold in the country north and east of us. A few years ago there was quite a gold excitement in the vicinity of North Western, and. we have heard recently that gold has been discovered in Lewis county. Word now comes that a plant for the extraction of gold from sand is to be erected on a certain farm in the town of Salisbury, Herkimer county.

All of this is very interesting and some people really have quite some confidence that gold will be found in paying quantity in the vicinity. At least they are willing to believe it enough to invest money, for the Salisbury plant is expected to cost about $10,000. Nevertheless, we have heard quite often after these experiments were made, that the gold (which undoubtedly is found) is in such small quantities and under such conditions that it does not pay to mine it.

In this connection it is interesting to recall one of these gold bonanzas which happened not many miles from here several years ago, a prospector took a party out to a field and there dug up some gold, or at least what was supposed to be gold. This mineral was sent to an assayer and was returned with the statement that it was not gold. The prospector, who found it, could not understand this, "because," said he, "I know it is gold. There isn't any doubt about it and I am positively sure." When asked how he "knew" it was gold he said he knew it because he "put it there himself." Of course that doesn't apply to any present day prospective undertakings. But at the same time it is worth while for those who are thinking of investing in gold prospects in this immediate vicinity to look over the situation—very—carefully—and—be sure that they don't need the money for some other purposes.

Rome Daily Sentinel, September 10, 1915

72

enough to make every human on earth a multi-millionaire. Obviously no one has figured out how to successfully get gold from the sea. However, in 1897, Rev. Prescott Jernigan, a Baptist clergyman, said he had a prophetic dream in which it was revealed to him how to harvest gold from seawater.

Jernigen convinced members of his church congregation and a number of his colleagues to sign on with him. The Electrolytic Marine Salts Company was formed in Boston, and before it was discovered that the divinely inspired Jernigen "sea gold accumulators" were bogus, the Reverend's flock lost hundreds of thousands of dollars. Gold and hucksters and victims. The Bre-X Factor.

The Bre-X Factor, as one would expect, figures noticeably into the search for gold in the North Country. The prospect of Adirondack millions, plus greed, plus cunning, all worked together to produce a smorgasbord of fraud. Sometimes it was interpersonal, sometimes corporate. Sometimes the fraud was unveiled and brought into the light. Sometimes it lay buried for a long, long time in dark mineshafts of the heart.

Gold fever is exactly that, a furiously infectious contagion. Just as a physiological disease has presenting symptoms so does the pathology of gold fever. The most prominent lesions are an utterly consuming obsession and, sooner or later, deceit and fraud.

On February 15, 1998, I followed Chief Carl Lane down the stairs to the basement of the Herkimer Police Station. Off in a corner there were several bookcases where turn-of-the-century records were stored. Together, Chief Lane and I looked at the arrest blotters for 1922. I found what I was looking for among the entries for May. On the 20th, Vasily Cherniak had indeed been arrested and sent to the Herkimer County Jail.

Cherniak was editor of a New York City, anti-Bolshevik newspaper called the *Golos-Rusi*, printed in Carpatho-Rusian. He was also president of the Oridio Platinum Gold Company, organized with a capitalization of $10,000,000.[2] Cherniak claimed to have discovered rich gold deposits on a southwestern Adirondack farm in Salisbury. As in the Bre-X scam, the big money would be made by selling worthless shares of Oridio stock.

And like Bre-X's Felderhof, Cherniak protested that he was innocent and that the rock samples taken from Salisbury soil were high in gold content: "Herkimer will one day be a great city. Our new process will solve the problem which has kept the ore from being mined for so many years. It has been known for a long time that gold was present in the rock formation, but engineers and experts have declared it impossible to extract the precious metal."[3] In post-bust Bre-X interviews Felderhof spoke from the safety of his Cayman Island villa; Cherniak, on the other hand, lauded his Oridio enterprise from a dank cell in the county lock-up. The next day he was taken to Westchester County where he was indicted for a similar gold scam in Yonkers.

I do not see the Salisbury gold scam as an amusing bit of local history. It is, rather, pretty sad commentary. Cherniak's victims were primarily poor Russian immigrants, suckered, via a language-friendly newspaper, into a sure way to obtain necessary finances for beginning a new life in America. "Cherniak and his promoters promised to pay $600 for each $1.00 investment in their scheme. Estimates of the money bilked from the victims range from $135,000 to $1,000,000."[4] The Bre-X Factor.

THE RIVERSIDE GOLD MINING
AND REDUCTION COMPANY

The Adirondack Museum was kind enough to send me a photocopy of a vintage North Country prospectus. It is a twelve-page booklet titled, *Prospectus of The Riverside Gold Mining and Reduction Company of St. Regis Falls, NY. Incorporated Under the Laws of the State of New York. Capital Authorized, $200,000. No. Of Shares, 40,000. Par Value, Five Dollars.*

The following excerpts provide a glimpse of Riverside's advertising style:

...The discovery of gold in apparently paying quantities in Franklin Co., N.Y., is not new nor the work of a day. It is due to D.M. Rieder, who as an expert, has for over five years, persistently devoted his entire time to prospecting, locating gold and silver claims, and filing the necessary papers with the secretary of state to become the owner of them. D.M. Rieder is not the only person to become convinced that this is a gold section. Preparations are being made by three large companies to sink shafts as soon as the weather will permit.... We estimate that every investor of twenty-five dollars ($25) at present prices, after three years will be placed in very comfortable circumstances the balance of his life. ...Prof. Fahrig (one of the most renowned assayers in the U.S.) states... that notwithstanding geologists' reports to the contrary, the region was right for great gold deposits, and that he would not be the least surprised to learn at any time of quartz being uncovered that would yield $1,000 per ton. Do not wait for personal solicitation but call or write at once for shares.[5]

"We Mean No Swindle," Maintains Cherniak Whom Police Discover

~~~ ~~~~st within 20 Minutes

ARRESTED IN PARIS FOR $100,000 MINING FRAUD UPON SCHENECTA~~~Y MAN

John Pincott and Arthur C~~~
They Are Honest Busi~~~
But Go to Jail—Crooks, ~~~
French Police.

Herkin
public c
on Chie
Patrolr
George
yester
the ar
tor of
Russ
428 F
Th
niak
lege
the
of ~~~
m~~~

Paris. May 3. (Associated Press.)
---With the arrest of John Pincott
and Arthur Ernest Cox here last
night, the French police claim to
have put to an end to the activities
of two international crooks, one of
whose last fields of endeavor was
New York state, where they sold
for $100,000 an option on a gold
mine to a wealthy citizen of
Schenectedy, whose name the
police withheld ~~~

okhout, principal School No.
ica. The entire program was
lows:
ection, "Glorianna," H. H. S.
estra; "America's Need of
" James S. Kittams, Ilion; "The
stman Substitute," Helen Nash,
le Falls; "Why Not Scrap Them
h'" Floyd Beattle, Little Falls;
ini's Keeper," Ruth Edgerton,
hawk; violin solo, "Salut
mour," Dorcas Read, Little
"Abraham Lincoln," Geoffrey
mer; "The Laughter of
Roberts, Ilion: "A
Allan Dodge,
Word," Irene
"Four
Her.
Cath-
"The
e La
y's Pick-
Dolge-

The New-York Times

A MAGNET FOR GOLD.
From the San Francisco Call.
TRUCKEE, June 21.—That certain
strated an attraction to-day in ~~~
of prom~~~ for gold ~~~

ALLEGED SALISBURY GOLD MINE FRAUD NIPPED WHEN PROMOTE~~~

Signor D'Alvear's Goldometer!

TREASURE FINDERS.

Various Forms of Scientific Appar-
atus for Locating Rich Lodes
of Precious Metal.

Magical devices for discovering deposits of precious metal are out of
fashion nowadays. Their place has
been taken by various contrivances of
a more or less scientific nature, by
means of which masses of gold and
silver, or rich lodes, may be located.
Most of these forms of apparatus are
elect~~~ the Philadelphia Saturday ~~~
One ~~~
iron ~~~
at a ~~~
thrus ~~~
to th ~~~
teleg ~~~
of th ~~~
mass ~~~
ly pa ~~~
sure ~~~
the c ~~~
Anot ~~~
staff ~~~
an in ~~~
Fo ~~~
much ~~~
sisti ~~~
rece ~~~
exac ~~~
that ~~~
If o ~~~
place ~~~
to is ~~~

sily C
reste~~~
Co~~~
mer, May
Vasily Ch
s Russi,
lishe
ew
terd
r, c
intec
is u
com
of ~~~
in
rs
t~~~
oter
to
to
of

GOLD FROM THE BRINY DEEP.

A New England Company Started with
$10,000,000 to Extract the Metal
from Salt Water.

NEWBURYPORT, Mass., Nov. 10.—The
Electrolytic Marine Salt Company has been
incorporated at Portland, Me., with a capital stock of $10,000,000. The purpose of the
company is to wrest from the sea the gold
that is held in solution, according to the
promoters' belief, by a jealously guarded
secret process. The discoverer of the won-
derful process by which the gold is to be
obtained is the Rev. P. F. Jernigan. He
says there is one grain of gold in each ton
of sea water, and by handling billions of
tons of the salty water the company expects to amass a fortune exceeding the div-
idends of the Standard Oil Trust.
The first installment of stock to be placed
on the market will comprise 100,000 shares.
The company proposes to place a large
block of the stock on the New York market.
On the coast of Maine there is an abandoned gristmill, which will be used by the ~~~

Signor D'Alvear has just arrived at New York,
from the Gold region of California, by way of
Panama, Chagres and New Orleans, bringing with
him a very large quantity of Gold ore, valued at
nearly one million dollars, which he collected there,
long before the Gold mines became known to the
residents of California generally.

In compliance with the interest of numerous
scientific gentlemen, Signor D'Alvear has
commenced the manufacture of his new Magnetic
Instrument, the *Goldometer,* which he offers for
sale, in the United States, for the remarkably low
price of Three Dollars each, accompanied by full
instructions for use, and a variety of Philosophical
hints drawn from the ancient and modern sciences,
or The Art of finding Mines of Gold, Platinum,
Quicksilver, Coal, Iron, Copper, Lead and other
Mineral Riches, the whole being given in a
publication called *The Gold Seekers's Guide....*

(Rome Daily Sentinel, 1-17-1849)

house
~~~ found
~~~ evidence, the
~~~ that steps have
~~~ provide "pay
~~~ospective custo-
~~~ending the ~~~

Gold deposits have actually been
found in Herkimer county, according
to authorities, but prospecting oper-
tions have shown that the gold is in K,"
a form not readily obtainable
"Mine" in Salisbury.
Herkimer, M~~~
mine~~~

~~~nts ~~~ouse on
already under provement
V. Rand St.,

South Fifth
ord Auto or
Observer-

Stock apparently sold like crazy and things seemed to be booming. Until two company officials, entrusted with all the company funds, went away, far, far away, on an equipment-purchasing trip. They were never heard of again.[6] In the end, the Riverside Gold and Reduction Company would die a Bre-X death.

In my prospecting trip for literary references to New York gold I kept coming across allusions to bunco enterprises associated with the "auriferous sands of the Adirondacks." A good example of a gold-sands scam involves the Waverly Reduction Company, an operation which is profiled in a 1912 *Sun* (New York) article:

> Promises of from 200 to 600 per cent profits, statements that the sand wastes of the Adirondacks contain millions upon millions of dollars worth of gold obtainable through secret processes, and encouraging and optimistic reports together with the linking of the name of Prof. Charles E. Locke of the Massachusetts Institute of Technology with the scheme have resulted in investment by many New England people in companies designed for the exploitation of the New York Ophir.[7]

The *Sun* story then quotes Edwin M. Jordan, operator of a "gold assaying laboratory" in Santa Clara, Franklin County and inventor of an "electro-magnetic" device capable of extracting gold from Adirondack gravel:

> The gold here is in very fine grains and is volatile. The application of great heat makes it dissipate into the air. My process extracts these fine grains and saves them. This process will extract gold from anything that contains it. Why, if we wanted to make a fortune we could extract gold from sea water. The Adirondacks have no attracttion for me. With this process I can go to the Yukon black sands deposit and get millions. Experiments I have made show a value of $3,000 to the ton. There is no limit to the wealth that can be obtained by it.[8]

Sadly, neither is there a limit to the capacity of men to rip one another off as they pursue their own golden dreams. As I reflect on the universality of the Bre-X Factor, I am reminded of a Mark Twain definition: "A gold mine is a hole in the ground with a liar at the top."

When it comes to gold and gold mining enterprises, the most savvy prospectors say, the only sure way to double your money is to fold it in the middle and put it right back in your pocket. The problem, as indicated by North Country history, is that common-sense advice is rendered mute and unintelligible when judgment and moral principle have been seduced by gold fever.

SAND GOLD AND GAS PROMOTIONS

Exchange Member Jewell Is to Leave Stock Exchange House.

MASSACHUSETTS INVESTS

Plant of the Gold Makers in Santa Clara Run by Altruist Jordan.

SPRINGFIELD, Mass., Feb. 23.—Promises of from 200 to 650 per cent. profits, statements that the sand wastes of the Adirondacks contain millions upon millions of dollars' worth of gold obtainable through secret recovery processes, and encouraging and optimistic "reports," together with the linking of the name of Prof. Charles E. Locke of the Massachusetts Institute of Technology with the scheme, have resulted in investment by many western New England people in companies designed for the exploitation of the New York Ophir. Most of the money has been invested in stock of the Waverly Reduction Company, promoted by Alfred E. Copp of 4 Post Office Square, Boston. Besides Col. W. F. Mason McCarty of New York, Copp has employed Edwin G. Jordan and others, on the strength of whose reports the local people have invested their money.

Many of the Springfield and western Massachusetts investors have bought stock through Oscar S. Greenleaf, a prominent resident of Springfield. Mr. Greenleaf is an enthusiast on the subject of Adirondack gold mining and believes there is "millions in it." So firm is his belief in the success of Jordan's scheme for the recovery of gold from sand that he shipped a quantity of Connecticut Valley sand to Jordan's laboratory in Santa Clara, Franklin county, N. Y., for experimentation, the theory being that the Adirondack sand is the result of glacial deposit and identical with the Connecticut Valley sand.

A year ago there was considerable interest among well known Springfield people in the Adirondack sand proposition, and a Springfield newspaper man was sent to Santa Clara to investigate the "secret process" for recovering gold from sand. The investigation was private and on the strength of it there was no public boom of the scheme. Since then prominent members of the Board of Trade have been importuned to invest and one of their number was commissioned to go to the Adirondacks and look into it. His report discourages associates from investing.

Jordan is an Englishman. His "secret process" of recovering gold from sand had as its basis the "radiomagnetic quality" of a secret composition he claimed to have accidentally discovered. This composition in the form of a plate at—

THE BRE-X FACTOR

"The Biblical axiom is, 'The love of money is the root of all evil.' Out of that axiom flows the Bre-X Factor: 'Any sustained period of gold fever will always produce bunco artists and victims.' Just as a physiological disease has presenting symptoms, so does the pathology of gold fever. The most prominent lesions are an utter consuming obsession and, sooner or later, deceit and fraud."

GOLD FROM SAND AND KERO GAS

Stock Exchange Members Find They Were Dealing With Ex-Convict

AND A WONDER MACHINE.

Supposed Plain Sand Yields Gold in the Manipulation.

SHARES FOR SALE? O, YES

1,954 Acres of Adirondack Barrens Figure as a Luscious Klondike.

STATE GEOLOGIST WARNS

Prospectus
—of—

The Riverside Gold Min and Reduction Co.,

—or—

St. Regis Falls, N. Y

Incorporated Under the Laws of the Sta New York.

—o—

Capital Authorized, $200,0

—o—

No. of Shares, 40,000.

—o—

Par Value, Five Dollars

Promoter of Gold Mine Under Arrest

WAS PLANNING OPERATIONS IN THE TOWN OF SALISBURY

Editor of New York Foreign Language Paper Nabbed at Herkimer—Charged With Complicity in Swindle at Yonkers—Had An Option on Part of Grassel Farm.

A passenger of evident foreign extraction alighted from a west bound Central train at the Herkimer depot Thursday afternoon, pointed out to a policeman in that vicinity another man who had also paid the train, and told the officer that the other man was wanted in Yonkers on a charge of conducting a $200,000 gold mine swindle. Then the mysterious stranger, after pointing to a clipping from a Russian language newspaper which told about the other fellow's alleged swindling operations, climbed back on the train.

The officer to whom the above information was imparted was Policeman Quirk. He reported the occurrence to Police Chief Keller and was detailed to shadow the man who had been pointed out to him. A little later the officer returned from this assignment and reported that the man had entered a house at 5 Malcolm street, Herkimer. The police of the county

been spent, so far as he knew. It is assumed that the sale of the stock in the Yonkers "gold mine" is the act on which the charges made against Cherniak at that city are based. He is alleged to have operated with five others in the sale of $200,000 worth of stock in the Yonkers mine. His accusers claim the stock is worthless.

The way Cherniak happened to become interested in the Salisbury proposition, he says, is that he became acquainted with Andrew Senyk, a Herkimer real estate dealer who advertised in the Cherniak paper. He came to Herkimer county and became interested in the Grassell land, on 20 acres of which he recently took an option. He insists there are fine opportunities for developing the property into a bonanza. His latest visit here, the prisoner said, was for the purpose of closing the option on the Salisbury land and making plans to get the mining operations there under

*The specimens you brought in are quite angular,
indicating that they have not traveled a great distance
from their source area, at least not by being water carried.
This mode of transport would round the grains rather
quickly. Transport by ice, would not, of course, but most
of the glacial material from the Adirondacks has not
traveled more than five miles. The bedrock in the area
from which the specimens came is metamorphosed
sedimentary and volcanic rock. It is conceivable that
this is the source. In any event, this occurrence of gold
raises some interesting geologic questions.*

—Dr. William Kelly, 1984
Curator of Minerals,
New York State Museum

—11—

The Cardiff Crock Principle

Like the Bre-X Factor, the Cardiff Crock Principle is directly related to the matter of North Country gold. Briefly stated, the Cardiff Crock Principle is this: "Absolute-sounding pronouncements by highly qualified geologists may or may not be based on accurate assumptions and therefore may or may not be worth a crock of beans."

In October 1869, some workmen were digging a well out behind Stub Newell's farm in Cardiff, N.Y. when they "discovered" a huge stone object of human likeness.

Neighbors and passersby helped unearth the "find," and soon the news was spreading like wildfire that the stone man, a.k.a. the Cardiff Giant, was either a petrified human or a statue of very great antiquity.

It subsequently came to light that this entire "archaeological event" was a hoax perpetrated by George Hull, Stub's brother-in-law, who lived in Binghamton. George, it turns out, had purchased a block of gypsum from Fort Dodge, Iowa, had gotten it carved by stone cutters in Chicago, and then had it shipped to Stub's farm where it was clandestinely interred until the day of the carefully orchestrated well-digging "find." It is not uncommon for authors and historians to refer to the Cardiff Giant scam as one of the most notorious hoaxes in American history.

The Cardiff Crock Principle, however, does not derive from the fraud aspect of the Cardiff Giant story, but rather from the extraordinary developments which immediately followed the unearthing of the "sleeping giant." In "The Cardiff Giant: A Chapter in the History of Human Folly," Andrew D. White, first president of Cornell University, describes how a "joy-in-believing frenzy spread to the community of the scholarly":

> ...a very excellent doctor of divinity, pastor of one of the largest churches in Syracuse, said very impressively, "Is it not strange that any human being, after seeing this wonderfully preserved figure, can deny

the evidence of his senses, and refuse to believe what is so evidently the fact, that we have here a fossilized human being, perhaps one of the giants mentioned in the Scripture."[1]

A beatific crock.

Even after being warned by not-so-frenzied colleagues, Dr. James Hall, Geologist for the State of New York, pronounced:

> To all appearance, the statue lay upon the gravel when the deposition of the fine silt or soil began, upon the surface of which the forests have grown for succeeding generations. Altogether it is the most remarkable object brought to light in this country, and although not dating back to the stone age, is, nevertheless, deserving of the attention of archaeologists.[2]

A scientific crock.

Professor White himself narrowly escaped embarrassment, he admits, only because a friend had managed to obtain an actual chunk of the giant, allowing for a close-up, thorough inspection. White tested the bit of stone with acid and found it "not hard carbonate of lime, but soft, friable sulphate of lime—a form of gypsum, which must have been brought from another part of the country."[3]

Prior to this, White had made an inaccurate assumption:

> One thing seemed to argue strongly in favor of its antiquity, and I felt bound to confess, to all who asked my opinion, that it puzzled me. This was the fact that the surface water flowing beneath it in its grave seemed to have deeply grooved and channeled it on the under side. Now the Onondaga gray limestone is hard and substantial, and on that very account is used in the locks upon the canals: for the running of surface water to wear such channels in it would require centuries.[4]

It appears that on his first visit to Cardiff (at least a week before he was given the test specimen), Professor White's compulsion to make a dignitary-level "pronouncement" overpowered the wiser route of thorough scientific inquiry. He was there in Stub's back yard, after all, as an authority. As such, even absent the data from any actual specimen, he went out on

At a Route 46 culvert a stream from the western escarpment of the Boonville Gorge spills into the Lansing Kill at the gorge's base. "What stuff had the glaciers dragged along with them in their formation? What things did they chew up in their retreat? When did all this take place? Could a prospector expect to find gold in the Boonville Gorge?"

a limb, chose to rely on his expertise at identifying minerals, and assumed the stone giant's composition to be Onondaga gray limestone. His assumption was dead wrong.

On a level far broader than the effect of surface water on Iowa gypsum, geologists have historically made huge, often divergent, assumptions about such processes as glaciation, mountain building, gorge cutting, volcanism, continent formation, and, fellow prospectors, mineral occurrence. Unlike, say, physics or chemistry, geology is based more on observations than experiments. And interpretation of these observations is always tied to beliefs, sometimes held almost religiously, about what the "primary" forces of geology really are.

For example, geologists of the "uniformitarian" persuasion hold that the record written in the rocks is the plain-truth result of known processes, occurring in a basically steady-state sort of way throughout eons of time. Such gradual processes are erosion, sedimentation, atmospheric cycles, and continental drift. However, geologists who stress "catastrophism" as the main engine of geology, hold an opposing view. They think the geological record can, and does, play tricks on its readers. For catastrophists, some phenomena which "appear" to have formed gradually, may in fact have been formed suddenly by things like asteroid impacts, or tsunamis, or massive "earthquakes" deep beneath the oceans.

Consider the Boonville Gorge, north of Rome, in the Adirondack foothills, a few miles from where my WC 12 students wrote tales about moody ghosts and miracle moss and lost gold mines. What forces made the gorge? What role was played by retreating glaciers? What stuff had the glaciers dragged along with them in their formation? What things did they chew up in their retreat? When did all this take place? What happened to the vast quantity of ice-melt water that lay in the great glacial Lake Port Leyden? For that matter, was there a great glacial Lake Port Leyden? Could a prospector expect to find gold in the Boonville Gorge?

A geologist's responses to any of these questions would depend on his assumptions, and it is clear to me that those assumptions flow from what are, at their core, almost sectarian-type beliefs about how geology works.

On August 3, 1980, the Utica *Observer-Dispatch* ran a feature story about gold in the Boonville Gorge. Francis Crumb, an *Observer-Dispatch* reporter, and Joseph Vincent, President of the Rome Historical Society decided to investigate whether prospector Peter Hugunine may have really found gold in the Gorge back at the turn of the century as he had claimed. They panned a stream that drained into the Lansing Kill, which flows at the base of the Gorge. They both found colors, took their finds to three jewelers and a precious metals specialist. The tiny nuggets were tested and found to be authentic gold. On March 30, 1998, I spoke with Francis Crumb on the phone and asked him how long it actually had taken him to find his gold. "Less than half an hour," he responded.

In that same *Observer-Dispatch* story is the following:

> Dr. Ingvar Isachsen, principal geologist for the New York State Museum of the State Education Department in Albany, was asked about the chance of finding gold in northern Oneida County. "It's about as close to impossible as can be," he said. "It's like getting oil in the Adirondacks."
>
> Isachsen said gold deposits tend to form in the upper levels of mountain ranges, and were formed millions of years ago about 25 miles below the surface—indicating that the mountains of today are in reality 25 miles below the original peaks.

"Whatever gold there was in the system has long since been eroded away," he said. Informed that flakes found in the Boonville Gorge had been verified as gold, Isachsen replied, "This is really a geological surprise. This is amazing. This is astonishing."

He added that there was a remote possibility the deposits were left eons ago by retreating glaciers.[5]

Enough said? When it comes to North Country prospecting, whether you are speculating on the contents of your gold pan, or the content of sources I have cited in these pages, or the content of a particular "scientific pronouncement," remember the Cardiff Giant and the Boonville Gorge.

Gold is where you find it.

The two materials most commonly mistaken for gold are fool's gold and yellow mica.

...Technically, fool's gold may be either of two minerals: pyrite [a sulphide of iron] or calchopyrite [a sulphide of copper and iron, and a major ore mineral of copper].

...Assuming that the [specimen] particle is on a flat surface, scrape it with the "flat" of a knife point and with some force, as if trying to make it stand on end. Pyrite will tend to "jump" under this pressure, away from the point, or may even fracture or fly apart, while calchopyrite and mica will immediately break up into many smaller pieces. Gold will flatten under such pressure, but will not break up into many smaller pieces.

The Rockhound's Manual
—Gordon S. Fay

—12—

Recreational Gold Panning and the DEC

In October 1997, my wife and I returned to North Lake where, in 1989, a few gold-looking flecks sparked the chain of events that would lead eventually to the sentences you are now reading. Things had changed. At the lake, that is. I still had, and have, the same canoe and the same wife. The canoe, though, now has fourteen years' worth of Adirondack adventures scratch-written into its gel-coat bottom.

In 1990, via a conservation easement acquired by the State of New York Department of Environmental Conservation (NYSDEC), with help from the Adirondack Nature Conservancy, 11,490 acres surrounding the upper end of North Lake were opened to the public. A well-maintained gravel road now extends along the entire western shoreline, and we were able to drive within half a mile of Ice Cave Creek.

Just off a large parking lot we slid our canoe into North Lake, mirror-like on this clear, windless day. In less than ten minutes we were at the mouth of Ice Cave Creek scouring the shores and the bottom for black sand or specks of promising glitter. We spent the afternoon paddling and panning for gold and drinking in deep the wilderness splendor around us. We didn't find anything exciting as far as colors go, but we had a grand time.

A week or so after this trip I was looking over a one-page DEC flyer titled, "Welcome To The North Lake Recreational Easement Lands." The brochure stated:

> Through the efforts of NYSDEC and Hancock Timber Resource Group, this land is managed for your use and enjoyment in a manner similar to the neighboring Forest Preserve. Recreational opportunities in this area include hiking, camping, horseback riding, hunting, fishing, nordic skiing, bicycling and canoeing.

I did not see, nor, of course, did I expect to see, gold panning among the allowable recreational opportunities. But the flyer sure got me to thinking about the legality of looking for gold on state land. On November 9, 1997, I sent the following letter to the DEC:

Frank M. Dunstan
Director
Division of Lands and Forests
50 Wolf Road
Albany, N.Y. 12233

Dear Mr. Dunstan,

I am a free lance writer working on a project about the search for gold in the Adirondacks. This correspondence to you derives from a discussion with Dr. William Kelly, State Mineralogist, and from a brief talk with Captain Paul Hartmann of the Herkimer DEC office. Both conversations took place 11-3-97.

I had asked Dr. Kelly about the legality of "recreational panning" for gold on state land. Dr. Kelly responded that in his 15-year tenure as State Mineralogist he has never gotten crystal clear light on that subject from the DEC.

Curious, I drove to Herkimer and met Captain Hartmann of the DEC. I told him that a few weeks ago I had been panning for gold along North Lake, Herkimer County, on state land.

Captain Hartmann felt unequivocally that as the State Constitution prohibits removal of material from state land and prohibits, as well, the disturbing of waterways, that panning was not legal. He said he would have been inclined to ticket me had he seen me engaging in the activity

Captain Hartmann expressed surprise that Dr. Kelly was not aware of relevant state law. I countered—as diplomatically as I dared, considering that I may have just confessed to a crime—that I surmised Dr. Kelly was aware of relevant state law as he, Dr. Kelly, some weeks prior had forwarded to me photocopies of statutes dealing with gold discovered on state land. Specifically, he sent me the Annotated Text of the Public Lands Law as Amended to June, 1993, Chapter 46 of the Consolidated Laws of the State of New York, Article 7.

Somewhat gingerly, I read Section 82, Subsection 4 to Captain Hartmann: "The filer (of the gold/silver notice of discovery sent to the Secretary of State per Section 82) shall have the benefit of minerals extracted from a mine or deposit on state land on the payment to the

86

state of such rental and such royalty as the commissioner shall deem reasonable."

At this point Captain Hartmann said there appeared to be a conflict within the Constitution and gave me your name as the person in a position to clarify things.

In an attempt to write you in a more focused, informed way, I have searched through Opinions of the Attorney General as recorded since 1791. I wanted to get a sense of how recreational gold panning might fit the historical interpretation of the Public Lands Law as it entwines with the Forest Preserve clause in the Constitution.

The Attorneys General waffled.

Early opinions allowed for the actual working of mines on state lands, including the Forest Preserve, so long as the timber was protected. The following thus illustrates: "Permission to erect buildings for working mines upon state lands within the Forest Preserve may be given by the forest commission and elsewhere by the commissioners of the land office, when such lands are entirely denuded of their timber." Attorney General Edward R. O'Malley to Hon. Samuel Koening, Secretary of State. 1910

Later opinions ruled that working a mine in the Forest Preserve is constitutionally barred: "The provisions of the Public Lands Law, section 80, et. Seq. in effect at the time the Forest Preserve clause (Article VII, section 7) was added to the Constitution, were abrogated and made null and void as to the State Forest Preserve, and any subsequent amendments or additions are ineffective. The project concerning which you inquire (working a deposit of gold and silver located in St. Lawrence County, inside the Blue Line) is not constitutionally allowable." Attorney General John J. Bennet, Jr. to the Conservation Commissioner. 1934

New York law is abundantly clear about who owns any deposit of gold or silver found anywhere in the state, whether on the Forest Preserve, or in my own back yard. The state owns it: "The following minerals are the property of the people of the state of New York in their right of sovereignty: (a) all deposits of gold and silver in or upon private lands and lands belonging to the people of the state of New York," Public Lands Law, Section 81.

As well, though, the law has historically made provision for the discoverer to benefit from his discovery of gold or silver, when given permission to mine by the land owner. "The right to remove mineral products is an incorporeal hereditament." Attorney General Bennet. 1934

The DEC, legitimately bowing to the transcendent Forest Preserve clause, can not, of course, give the necessary permission to work a mine on forest preserve land. (This was Bennet's clear conclusion.)

However, current law still states that any discoverer of gold or silver upon state land, even within the Forest Preserve, may file a notice of discovery with the Secretary of State: "...in my opinion the Secretary of State has no discretion to refuse to file a notice of discovery simply upon the ground that the mine is located upon such lands" (Forest Preserve). Attorney General O'Malley. 1910

The above opinion must still hold, for the Secretary of State continues to officially accept notices of discovery of gold and silver upon Forest Preserve lands. Some of these more recent claims are held in Miscellaneous Records, NYS Department of State, 41 State Street, third floor.

Here is my layman's reasoning: "Discovery" must be preceded by some kind of "looking for," whether the find is a result of a fortuitous glimpse at a shining speck, or an intentional search. And "discovery," per statue, is followed by the filing of a notice of discovery, which the Secretary of State is obliged to accept. The very process itself upholds the idea that a U.S. citizen has a right to discover gold anywhere within New York State, so long as he is not criminally trespassing when he makes the discovery.

He does not own the gold. He may not ever be able to mine it. But he has the legal right to discover it and to file formal notice of his discovery. This much seems to be well established by legal precedent. What I am writing you about, however, is the "looking for" part of this matter.

Within the Forest Preserve a person may "discover" a splendid brook trout on the end of his fishing line. Or he may "discover" the perfect walking stick, one end gnawed a summer ago by a beaver, the other end beautifully whittled by its most recent human owner. Or he may "discover" a dear antler (trace amounts of gold are found in deer antlers, by the way), or a silvery gray piece of drift wood, or a porcupine quill, or a goose feather, or maybe just the one needed crimson maple leaf to complete the third-grade bulletin board.

Or, he may discover... gold.

The matter before us, before Captain Hartmann and me anyway, is to what degree the DEC will let someone intentionally look for gold. The "DEC codes and Regulations" do not seem to address recreational prospecting. There is, however, a definition of mining: mining means "The extraction of minerals from the earth to make them suitable for sale or exchange, or for commercial, industrial, municipal, and construction use." Section 420.1, subsection k, Title 6, Environmental Conservation.

Therein lies, it seems, the important distinction between "working a deposit or mine" and recreational/educational panning for gold.

As you probably know, federal policy allows for recreational prospecting within federal parks, so long as the environment is not harmed in any way.

Having shared with you some of my reading and some of my thinking, I would now ask you for your position on the following three questions:

(1) Dr. Kelly has in his office a tiny specimen of gold taken from an Adirondack lake by a professional New York historian and his wife as they were "panning for gold." Is Dr. Kelly in possession of stolen property?

(2) There are hundreds of New York rockhounds who may have in their collections specimens taken from inside the Blue Line. Have such fledgling geologists and field-tripping earth science students engaged in acts forbidden by law and punishable upon conviction?

(3) Would you advise Captain Hartmann to ticket me if he should find me panning for gold again on state land?

Sincerely,
Ronald Johnson

On January 7, 1998, Frank Dunstan informed me that my letter had been referred to the DEC Division of Legal Affairs. Several weeks later I received the following response, printed here with (NYSDEC) Senior Attorney Hamm's permission:

New York State Department of Environmental Conservation
Division of Legal Affairs, Room 638
50 Wolf Road
Albany, New York 12233-1500
Telephone (518) 457-8809; Facsimile (518) 457-3978

JOHN P. CAHILL
COMMISSIONER

February 2, 1998

Mr. Ronald Johnson
1812 Culver Court
Utica, NY 13501

Dear Mr. Johnson:

This responds to your November 9, 1997 letter to Frank Dunstan regarding the legality of recreational panning for gold on state land. Mr. Dunstan referred you letter to me for a response, as I am the program attorney for the Division of Lands and Forests. I apologize for the delay in responding to your letter.

I will respond to your questions in the order in which they were posed:

1. Dr. Kelly has in his office a tiny specimen of gold taken from an Adirondack lake by a professional New York historian and his wife as they were "panning for gold." Is Dr. Kelly in possession of stolen property?

It is not clear from your question whether the lake in question was in State or private ownership. I assume from your question that the lake in question is in State ownership and is classified as Forest Preserve land.

No statute or regulation prohibits the act of recreational gold panning on State lands, regardless of the classification of the land. No permit from the Department is needed to engage on State lands in a wide variety of passive recreational activities, such as hiking, birdwatching, canoeing, and camping. Similarly, it would appear that an individual may, without a permit, recreationally pan for gold on State lands under this Department's jurisdiction in a manner which does not disturb the environment.

However, 6 NYCRR §190.8(g) prohibits the removal of any rock, fossil, or mineral found on State land except by permit from the Commissioner of Environmental Conservation and the Assistant Commissioner for State Museum and Science Service pursuant to Education Law 233. This statute does not authorize the issuance of permits for private purposes. Since the regulation provides no de minimis exception to this permit requirement, removal of even a "tiny specimen" without the requisite permits would violate 6 NYCRR §190.8(g).

2. There are hundreds of New York rockhounds who may have in their collections specimens taken from inside the Blue Line. Have such fledgling geologists and field-tripping earth science students engaged in acts forbidden by law and punishable upon conviction? Initially I should note that lands inside the "blue line" include a mixture of both private and State lands. I again assume that your question relates to State lands.

Rockhound activities are not regulated by this Department so long as their activities are confined to finding minerals without disturbing the soil, and no sale or exchange of minerals results. However, again note that 6 NYCRR §190.8 (g) prevents rockhounds from removing their finds from State land without the requisite permits.

3. Would you advise Captain Hartmann to ticket me if he should find me panning for gold again on state land? Captain Hartmann would be advised to do his job based upon the circumstances which he observes. One would expect that his reaction would vary with those circumstances.

As an additional note, please be advised that your recreational panning would have to be conducted on a scale small enough so as not to disturb the waters of state (the stream/lake used for panning) and subject you to penalties associated with violations of Article 15 of the Environmental conservation Law. Nor would you be permitted to cause discharges of pollutants into the streams or lakes during your panning activities.

I trust that this answers your questions.

Sincerely,

Kenneth R. Hamm

Kenneth R. Hamm
Senior Attorney

cc: F. Dunstan

There you have it, about as official as can be. You can pan for gold, without a permit, on state-owned land so long as you do it in a way that does not harm the environment and so long as you follow the mining regulations of the Public Lands Law and the DEC. On Forest Preserve land you can also pan for gold without a permit, but you cannot take any colors you find with you. Nor, apparently, can you legally remove from the Forest Preserve any other mineral, even in trace quantities, including the mud on your boots and the wild strawberries in your food tube, as the pertinent regulations contain, according to Hamm, no "de minimus exception."

Alas, the trials and tribulations of Adirondack prospecting. The ruggedness of the mountains. The black flies. The historical odds. The mutterings of concerned friends in their right minds. The Bre-X Factor. The Cardiff Crock Principle. And to top it all off, the Forest Preserve De Minimus Absurdity.

Essentially all of the gold found in New York has been located within the Adirondack Mountains in the northern part of the state. These mountains are among the oldest in the world and have exhibited positive relief throughout much of the geological record. Crystalline rocks within this province do contain gold-bearing quartz veins, but up to the present all mining ventures have been unable to find commercial reserves.

—Gold Prospector, April 1987

—13—

Madness at Star Lake

The following appeared in the *New York Times*, July 5, 1896:

GOLD IN THE ADIRONDACKS

Utica, July 4 — The effort now being made to extract gold from the sands of Fulton County, at Gloversville, is another attempt to unlock the mystery of the gold fields of Northern New York. For half a century, at least, men have lived who have had implicit faith in their existence, and years of toil and anxious search have been spent, and many thousands of dollars have been expended by those who were led forward by the great hope that they would be the ones to locate and develop mines as rich in the mineral for which all nations are striving as any this country has ever produced.

There is not a guide in the whole Adirondack region who has not dreamed at some time of stumbling across the fabled Golconda, and of coming forth in the end to astonish the world with his riches. Around every campfire for a score of years stories of lost mines have been told to those who came to spend a few nights in the woods, and with whom intimate acquaintances were formed. There are in the North Woods today men who were led to give up active business and professional lives and pursue the calling of guides, trappers, and hunters, hoping that they might be the fortunate ones to open these veins of gold-bearing quartz, which have here been located by the legends of the campfire. Though they have been disappointed in their years of search, there is not one of them who does not implicitly believe in the lost gold mines of the Adirondacks.

Five years ago last August, in a little cabin at the foot of Twin Lakes, the story that follows was told by a trapper and guide named Ike Wilson. The following spring he was killed by the fall of a tree that had been loosened by the frosts and thaws. He had been in the woods since boyhood, and his knowledge of the great tract was intimate. Moreover, he bore a record of truthfulness, and the manner in which he related the tale convinced his hearers that he was not dealing in fiction:

"It was four years ago this summer," said Ike, "and I had a cabin at Star Lake. My partner had gone out for some supplies, and one day along came a couple of strangers, who said they wanted a guide to steer them a day's journey into the woods from the lake. They had heard about the magnetic iron ore in those parts, and, though they had a good compass, they were afraid to trust the instrument for fear of variation of the needle. I had just come out with a party of hunters and the newcomers wanted me to guide them. They spent a day getting the points of the compass, and in consulting a little map which one of them carried. When we started we first went up on Bald Mountain, near Star Lake, and they drew a straight line on the map and said they wanted to follow that. It ran a little to the right of Bald Mountain, and in the direction where the guides seldom went at that time, and where I had never been.

"They were packed very light, and the only weapons they had were revolvers. Of course I knew that they were neither fishermen nor hunters, and, though we were used to all sorts of prospectors in those days, there were mysterious movements about these two that I didn't like. They wanted me to run out the line and blaze the trail. Then I could return, they said, and they could take care of themselves for four or five days. I explained that it would not be business-like to leave them in that way, and hinted at the light provision packs, and absence of guns, the danger of being lost in the timber, and the certain fate that awaited them. They allowed that they understood all the chances, and that it was no concern of mine so long as I did my part of the work. I finally agreed to blaze the line for them, and we started out at daylight the next morning.

"They were in high feather when we camped that night, and for a long time they studied the map by firelight and talked together in whispers. We were then about eighteen miles from Star Lake, and the next morning we went about three miles more. Then they called a halt and told me it was time for me to go back. Again I warned them of the danger of being lost. I showed them how the magnetic ores in that region played mischief with the needle, and pointed out the uniform appearance of the timber in every direction. I made them promise to blaze any trail they should make from the little bark hut we built there, and told them how men lost in the woods follow circles until exhausted or starved. They did not seem to understand my anxiety, and appeared to take it as none of my concern, anyway. So I left them and returned to the lake.

"The next day I went out with a party of fishermen to Cranberry

Lake. We were gone ten days, and I kept worrying about the strangers all the time. When we got back to Star Lake I learned nothing had been heard of them, and I made up my mind they were lost. I knew they had a scant four days' rations, and no weapons but pistols with which to kill game. I talked it over with my partner, and the next morning before daylight we started to run over the trail. The blaze marks were plain, and we followed them rapidly.

"When we were within a mile of the hut where I left them we came upon the body of the younger man. He had apparently started along the trail to Star Lake, and had fallen and died within a mile of the hut. He was wasted almost to a skeleton. We covered the body with some branches and hurried forward to the hut, and there, lying on the dirt floor and raving in the delirium that goes before death from starvation, was the other stranger. In his right hand he clutched this little piece of rock."

The old guide took from his knapsack a piece of rock half as big as a hen's egg and passed it around for the inspection of his listeners. It was dark colored, very heavy, and was streaked with veins of ultramarine blue. There were no members of the party who ever examined ores, and therefore no opinion was expressed concerning it. Wilson said that men who claimed to know had assured him it was a rich specimen of gold-bearing rock. He carefully wrapped it in a piece of deerskin and continued his story:

"We gave him some pieces of crackers soaked in whiskey and water, and after an hour or so he stopped raving so badly. He was very weak, however, and I was fearful from the start that he would not live many hours. From his half-rational talk we gathered that he had been a Colorado prospector, and the other man was a mining expert. They had got some clue to a gold mine in this section from a man they met in Colorado, and had come east to locate and claim it. After I had left them they followed the descriptions on their map, and after a search of four days they found the outcroppings of rock, which astonished both by its apparent value, as it was richer than they had ever seen before. The fifth day was spent in getting out a claim. By this time their provisions had exhausted, and they could not kill any game with their pistols. They attempted to blaze a trail back to their hut, but their compass failed them, and they wandered day after day, they knew not where. One day they killed a rabbit, and were so crazed by hunger that they fought over the body. Their tools and packs were discarded, and they stumbled blindly along until they fell from exhaustion. Then, when they had rested, they would rise and press forward. The night before we came they had by mere chance stumbled upon the hut, and that morning the younger man had started out to follow my trail to Star Lake.

"He told no connected story, but this we guessed at from the few intelligent words he spoke at long intervals, and from his constant ravings and mutterings. Nor could we gain any idea as to the direction of their rich discovery, but I judged that it must have been at least ten or fifteen miles.

"We did all we could for him, but he was too far gone to rally, and along in the night he died. In his ravings he called the name of John and Eggleston very often, so we made up our minds that the younger man's name was John Eggleston. He also spoke often about 'the boys at Georgetown,' and frequently remarked, 'This beats Colorado.' Most of his talk was about pay rock, and once he rose from the floor and shouted: 'Here it is Eggleston! Here it is! Pay rock, as sure as God!'

"He held the little specimen I showed you till the last, and I took it from his hands just before we buried him. Any papers or money they may have had must have been in their packs, for we found nothing on either body to identify them. We wrote to Georgetown, Col., and inquired about John Eggleston, but were told the name was not known there."

"Have you ever made any attempt to find the mine?" the guide was asked.

"Yes; twice. Pardner and I were there two different times, but were not prepared to stay long enough to hunt it up. Besides that, we didn't know anything about what kind of rock to look for, and might have stumbled over 'pay rock' a dozen times and not have known it. We came upon the trail they had tried to be made up of mixed circles that went no place the last time we went. We found one of their hatchets, one pistol, and a piece of brown paper, in which were two more pieces of rock like the one I showed you. A red cotton handkerchief was tied around the paper to carry it by.

"The next winter my pardner died and I have never been in that section since. Some time a big party with lots of experienced men with lots of supplies and plenty of money to spend for more, will go in and solve the mystery of the Star Lake region. I ain't the only man in the woods who believes that there is a treasure there worth looking for. Few believe, however, that it will ever be found by those who are searching for it, but that it must wait to be stumbled upon by accident. They are superstitious, and they say that disaster has come to every man who has tried to make the discovery."

A golden bridge flanked by lions of gold leads to a third tower, covered with gold. This is where the Khmer god-king lives. When he comes out, the cavalry leads the escort. Then come the goat carriages and the horse carriages, all ornamented with gold. The king stands on a huge elephant whose tusks are wrapped in gold. The king's escorts carry twenty gold decorated parasols of white silk with golden handles.

—Chou Ta-kuan
Chinese trade emissary to Cambodia, 1296 A.D.

If I have made gold my hope, or have said to the fine gold, Thou art my confidence; If I rejoiced because my wealth was great, and because mine hand hath gotten much; If I beheld the sun when it shined, or the moon walking in brightness; And my heart hath been secretly enticed, or my mouth hath kissed my hand: This also were an iniquity to be punished by the judge: for I should have denied the God that is above.

Job 31:24-28
King James Version of the Bible

—14—

Union Station

The search for gold in the Adirondacks is tied, always, to the values and motivations of the searchers. Gold fever, the Bre-X Factor, even recreational gold panning, all connect at some level to men's hearts and the notions of "treasure" and of "the good life" that reside there.

The literature about New York gold is rich with stories of driven prospectors and gullible investors whose lives were shredded by dreams and schemes of quick and easy wealth. Some life-long prospectors, though, apparently saw gold for what it was, and so escaped the ravages of full blown gold fever.

Take Peter Hugunine, the fellow, you remember, who in the early 1900s discovered gold in the Boonville Gorge. I had judged from newspaper articles that he was most likely an obsessed goldhound, consumed, greedy, eccentric, reclusive. Then one day I walked into the headquarters of the Rome Historical Society and looked up at the foyer wall. Hanging there was a famous 5' x 7' painting of Fort Stanwix. The artist was Peter Hugunine, whose great grandfather fought in the Battle of Oriskany.

An obituary held by the Society stated that Hugunine played the clarinet, the cornet, and the violin, and gave lessons in each, and for years was a member of the band in Rome. Several newspaper stories reported that Hugunine actually took some gold from one of his finds and crafted a necklace for a lady friend. Peter F. Hugunine, the obituary said, was a man of fine character and much talent, esteemed by all. He was, evidently, a person who had spent a great deal of his sixty-five years searching for North Country gold, but he had left a lot of room in his life for art and music and courting and even a bit of goldsmithing.

"Goldsmithing." A good bridge to one last thing I want to share with you about gold. Though the following story has its genesis in Southeast Asia, there is a lesson in gold assaying that is of singular and universal importance, a lesson learned in an abyss of sorrow and evil. See this brief

99

sketch of a Cambodian goldsmith, perhaps, as one last trowel-full of gravel to run through your sluice.

Utica, southwestern gateway to the Adirondack Mountains, is about fifty miles from Ice Cave Creek. In the 1980s Utica was one of a dozen United States relocation centers for Cambodian refugees. At the time, I was teaching English as a Second Language at Mohawk Valley Community College on the city's east side. I happened to be called upon, in the spring of 1981, to help a Cambodian gentleman whose language difficulty was causing a huge medical problem. The fellow's name was In Chhan and we became very good friends.

The director of the refugee center told me some details of In Chhan's ordeal. Throughout the early 1970s a madman named Pol Pot had been abducting Cambodian children from the countryside. He took them deep into the jungle and he ruthlessly brainwashed them. On April 17, 1975, Pol Pot's Khmer Rouge (Red Cambodian) youth became mindless killing machines. Wearing red headbands and armed with AK-47s, axes, clubs, and plastic bags (for suffocating enemies of the new regime) they stormed into the Cambodian capital, Phnom Penh, and force-marched two million residents out of the city.

The mass killings began right along with the mass exodus. In the end, the killing fields of Cambodia would claim over two-million lives, and *Time* magazine would have to invent a new word: auto-genocide.

On that same horrible day, April 17, 1975, In Chhan, his wife, and their seven children joined the hellish march out of Phnom Penh to nowhere. The day before, he had been a wealthy goldsmith. Now, any attempt to retrieve his gold, or even mention it, would mean certain execution.

One night In Chhan and his whole family escaped from a slave labor camp into the jungle. Against formidable odds they found their way to the Thai border. They were eventually granted refugee status by Congress and were flown to Utica via the Philippines. After about a year in Utica, In Chhan decided to move to Long Beach, California, another Cambodian refugee relocation center. He asked if I would take him to the train station. I shall never forget that evening. In Chhan's wife and children boarded the train. Then he climbed the first step, stopped abruptly, turned and looked into my eyes.

In a voice breaking with emotion he said, "Mr. Ron, I never talk you about before but must tell now. In Cambodia, before Pol Pot, I goldsmith. I rich man. I have much, much gold. But I not have God in my heart, so I

"Just north of Union Station, where a good and noble Cambodian friend told me of gold lost and gold found, there is a rise of land. Beyond the rise lies the great Adirondack wilderness, ancient beaver hunting ground of the Iroquois. The fur trade had died, but never the quest for North Country wealth. That same vast tract of land would become, for more than two centuries, the ever-alluring gold hunting ground for countless folks who sought to realize their various perceptions of treasure by romancing the stones."

poor. Now, my gold all gone, but have my wife and have my family and have God in my heart and, Mr. Ron, I rich, rich man." He waved goodbye and then disappeared inside the passenger car. The sleek silver train rolled out of the station and was soon speeding westward into an April sunset.

Just north of Union Station, where a good and noble Cambodian friend told me of gold lost and of gold found, there is a rise of land. Beyond the rise lies the great Adirondack wilderness, ancient beaver hunting ground of the Iroquois. The fur trade had died, but never the quest for North Country wealth. That same vast tract of land would become, for more than two centuries, the ever-alluring gold hunting ground for countless folks who sought to realize their various perceptions of treasure.

I have now shared with you the colors of my own prospecting adventure. But, fellow panners and miners and truth-seekers, the romance need not be over for us. We've certainly not turned over every last stone. Intriguing questions remain. Is there more to be learned about the source of the Fort Orange golden face paint? What in the world were the Beldens hauling out of the Adirondacks by sealed barrel and box in the middle of the night and taking to the Amsterdam train station? What is the source of the gold that shows up in the Moose River? Can we figure out where Peter Hugunine found gold in the Boonville Gorge? What happend to the "reserve of gold" in Macomb's Purchase that is documented in *Opinions of the Attorneys General*? Did the Star Lake logger who discovered a "mile long" vein of gold in the town of Fine have any luck staking and working his claim? Beckoning queries like these abound.

As for me, come spring, I plan to scratch another story or two onto the hull of my canoe. You guessed it. North Lake. I'm going to follow Ice Cave Creek to its source, panning along the way, and then I'm going to tramp Ice Cave Mountain in search of Dingle Dangle's mine. As I type these last lines I feel the thrill of another great hunt taking hold.

Perhaps I'll see you downstream. I'm okay with that. The North Country is plenty big enough for all of us who are tugged from the mundane by tantalizing tales of mountain glitter.

ENDNOTES

CHAPTER 2

1. John Mylod, *Biography of a River* (New York, Hawthorne, 1969). p.21.
2. Roland Van Zandt, *Chronicles of the Hudson* (New Jersey: Rutgers University Press, 1971), p. 7.
3. Robert Juet, "The Third Voyage of Master Henry Hudson," as translated and reproduced in *Narratives of New Netherland, 1609-1664* (New York: Scribners, 1909), pp. 18, 20, 25, 26, 27.
4. Tristram Coffin, *The Lost Gold Mine of the Hudson* (New York: Knickerbocker Press, 1915), p. 20.
5. Ibid.
6. Henry Collins Brown, *The Story of Old New York* (New York: E. P. Dutton, 1934), p. 40.

CHAPTER 3

1. Isaac Jogues, "A Description of New Netherland in 1644" as reproduced by E.B. O'Calloghan, *The Documentary History of the State of New York* (New York: Weed and Parsons, 1850-1851), Vol. IV, pp. 15-16.
2. Francis Talbot, S.J., *Saint Among Savages* (New York: Harper, 1935, p. 412.
3. Ibid.
4. George Huesser, *Gold, Silver and Other Mines of the Shawangunks* (Ellenville, New York: Huesse, 1976).
5. Francis Talbot, S. J., p. 399.
6. Ibid.

CHAPTER 4

1. Adriaen Van der Donck, *A Description of the New Netherlands, 1656*, translated by Hon. Jeremiah Johnson, 1841, reproduced in *Collections of the New York Historical Society* (New York: H. Ludwig, 1841), Vol. I, pp. 160-161.
2. David De Vries, from *Korte Historiael End Journaels Aenteyckeninge, 1655*, translated by Henry C. Murphy, reproduced in *Original Narratives of New Netherlands* (New York: Barnes and Noble, 1967), pp. 228-229.
3. Adrian Van der Donck, pp. 160-161.
4. Arnoldus Montanus, *Description of New Netherland, 1671*, translated from the Dutch, published by E.B. O'Calloghan, Ed. (New York:Weed and Parsons, 1850-1851), Vol. IV, pp. 46-47.

5. Patricia Edwards Clyne, *Hudson Valley Tales and Trails* (Woodstock, New York: Overlook Press, 1990).

6. Rollin G. Osterweis, *Three Centuries of New Haven* (New Haven: Yale University Press, 1951), pp. 46-47.

7. Adrian Van der Donck, p. 162.

8. Rollin G. Osterweis, p. 47.

9. Cotton Mather, *Magnalia Christi Americana*, 1853 Edition, Vol. I.

10. Henry Wadsworth Longfellow, "The Phantom Ship," *The Complete Poetical Works of Henry Wadsworth Longfellow*, (Boston: Houghton Mifflin, 1893), pp. 187-188.

11. *The Representation of New Netherland, 1650*, translated from the Dutch by Henry C. Murphy, as printed in Original Narratives of New Netherland, 1609-1644 (New York, Weed and Parsons, 1856), Vol. I, p. 299.

12. E. B. O'Calloghan, *Documents Relating to the Colonial History of the State of New York* (New York: Weed and Parsons, 1856), Vol. I., p. 262.

CHAPTER 5

1. Tharrett Gilbert Best, *Boonville and Its Neighbors* (Boonville, New York: Willard Press, 1961), p. 24.

2. Theobold Clark, "Treasure Roundup," *North Country Life*, Spring, 1950, p. 45.

3. Gilbert Hagerty, *Wampum, War and Trade Goods West of the Hudson* (Interlaken, New York: Heart of the Lakes Publishing, 1985), p. 101.

4. Ibid., p. 111.

5. Ibid., p. 110.

CHAPTER 6

1. Willis Fletcher Johnstone, *Political and Governmental History of the State of New York* (Syracuse: Syracuse University Press, 1922), Vol. I., pp. 39-40.

2. John G. Bennet, Jr., *Opinions of the Attorney General, 1934*, p. 283.

3. Personal telephone interview.

4. Howard Thomas, *Folklore From the Adirondack Foothills* (Prospect, New York: Prospect Press, 1958), p. 77.

5. Howard Thomas, *Tales From the Adirondack Foothills* (Prospect, New York, Prospect Press, 1956), p. 99.

6. Annotated Text of Public Lands Law as Amended to June, 1993, Chapter 46 of the Consolidated Laws of the State of New York, Article VII, Sec. 81.

7. Ibid., Sec. 82.

8. Department of (New York) State, *Report of the Attorney General of New York, 1947*, p. 268.

CHAPTER 7

1. As cited by Elizabeth Folwell, "Adirondack Eldorado," *Adirondack Life,* January-February, 1993, p. 19.

CHAPTER 8

1. J.N. Nevius, "The Sacandaga Milling Co. and the 'Sutphen Process,'" *New York State Museum, Report of the Director, 1898,* Report 52, Vol. I, pp. 182-187.
2. Memoranda, New York Secretary of State, Form 170.5, 7-3-17-100 (2-7617).
3. "Gold in the Adirondacks*," Engineering and Mining Journal*, April 2, 1910. p. 695.
4. *Ogdensburg Journal*, December 7, 1922.
5. D.H. Newland, "The Prospect of Gold in New York State," New York State Museum Circular 12, February 1933.
6. James F. Davis, "Golden Dreams," New York State Museum newsletter, undated.
7. Jim McGuire, "Thar Still Is Gold In Then Thar Hills," *Schenectady Gazette,* February 8, 1984.
8. Andy Maslowski, "Gold in New York State," *Gold Prospector*, April 1987, p. 23.

CHAPTER 9

1. *Gloversville Daily Leader*, October 5, 1896.
2. Frederick C. Aber and Stella King, *History of Hamilton County* (Boonville, New York: Willard Press, 1965), p. 130.
3. John J. Bennet, Jr., *Opinions of the Attorney General, 1947*, p. 282.
4. G. Byron Bowen, Editor, *History of Lewis County*, New York (Boonville, New York: Willard Press, 1970), pp. 431-432.
5. "The Adirondack Gold Mines," *Gloversville Intelligencer*, June 29, 1882.
6. Elizabeth Folwell, "Adirondack Eldorado," *Adirondack Life*, January-February, 1993, p. 19.
7. "About a Gold Mine in Ava," *Rome Daily Sentinel*, September 12, 1904.
8. Warwick S. Carpenter, "Lure of the Adirondack Gold*," The Outing Magazine*, February, 1911, Vol. 57, pp. 522-532.
9. George Alan Sturla, "Some Adirondack Tales of the 'Brick' Variety*," The Pine Log*, March, 1925, pp. 8-10, 25-27.
10. *Amsterdam Evening Journal*, August 3, 1880.
11. "Our Gold Fields," *Gloversdale Daily Leader*, September 18, 1898.

12. "Finding Gold in New York State," *Scientific American*, March 26, 1898.
13. "Gold in the Upper Valley," *Rome Daily Sentinel*, August 12, 1905.
14. "Gold," *Gloversville Intelligencer*, February 1, 1983.
15. Gordon S. Fay, *The Rockhound's Manual* (New York: Harper and Row, 1972), pp. 104-106.
16. "A Gold Mine at Hand," *Rome Daily Sentinel*, July 29, 1904.
17. "The Adirondack Eldorado," *Albany Evening Journal*, December 28, 1882.
18. Frederick C. Aber and Stella King, p. 127.
19. Ibid., p.128.
20. "Wealth in Rugged Rocks," *Rome Daily Sentinel*, December 8, 1906.
21. Ted Aber, *Adirondack Folks* (Prospect New York: Prospect Press, 1980), p. 11.
22. Paul Warloski, "Logger Stakes Claim To Adirondack Gold Discovered While Scouting Near Star Lake," *Watertown Times*, January 20, 1992.

CHAPTER 10

1. Anthony Spaeth, "The Golden Shaft," *Time*, May 19, 1997, p. 58.
2. *Utica Daily Press*, May 20, 1922.
3. Ibid.
4. James F. Davis
5. Photocopy of *Riverside Goldmining and Reduction Company Prospectus*, Courtesy of Adirondack Museum.
6. Ralph M. Farmer, "The Riverside Gold Mining Company," courtesy of Adirondack Museum.
7. *The Sun* (New York City), February 25, 1912.
8. Ibid.

CHAPTER 11

1. Andrew D. White, "The Cardiff Giant: A Chapter in the History of Human Folly—1869-1870," as reprinted by A.`M. Drummond and Robert E. Gardin in *The Cardiff Giant* (Ithaca, New York: Cornell University Press, 1949), p. 103.
2. Ibid., p. 104.
3. Ibid., pp. 105-106.
4. Ibid., p. 101.
5. Francis L. Crumb, "Yep, There's Really Gold in Them Thar Hills," *Utica Observer-Dispatch*, August 30, 1980.

About the Author

Ron Johnson taught English 12 at Adirondack Central School, Boonville, New York, from 1968 to 1975. He and his wife, Donna, then taught for four years at Okinawa Christian School, Okinawa, Japan. Upon their return to the U.S., Ron taught English as a Second Language at Mohawk Valley Community College. From 1981 to 1989 he served as director of the men's program at the Utica Rescue Mission. It was at this time that he began free-lance writing, contributing to a number of publications.

Ron is currently an adult education instructor with Madison-Oneida County BOCES and teaches classes in literacy, citizenship, and English as a Second Language at the Arc of Oneida-Lewis County and at the Mohawk Valley Resource Center for Refugees. If he is asked about his joys in life, his response is immediate and unequivocal: two fine sons. Ron's hobbies are wilderness camping and sailing, but he says the supreme delight is taking a first-timer on a North Woods adventure, or passing the tiller and the main sheet to a neophyte, thereby instantly transfusing the goose-bump thrill of owning the wind that fills your sail.